TOWN & VILLAGE DISCOVERY TRAILS

Cumbria & the Lake District

Norman Buckley

Published by Sigma Leisure – an imprint of
Sigma Press, 1 South Oak Lane, Wilmslow, Cheshire SK9 6AR, England.

British Library Cataloguing in Publication Data
A CIP record for this book is available from the British Library.

ISBN: 1-85058-482-6

Typesetting and Design by: Sigma Press, Wilmslow, Cheshire.

Cover Design: MFP Design & Print

Cover Photograph: High Cross, Appleby (June Buckley)

Photographs: June Buckley

Maps: Elizabeth Fowler

Printed by: MFP Design & Print

Preface

This book is intended to stimulate interest in twenty-three selected towns and villages throughout Cumbria by highlighting their features, firstly by a general description and then by suggesting a walking route or "trail" which links those features.

Whilst the time required to complete a trail can be as long or as short as anyone cares to linger, and will obviously be extended if any of the indoor attractions such as galleries and museums are visited, the guiding principle has been that one to one and a half hours will normally allow a reasonable appreciation of most towns and villages. In no case is strenuous or lengthy walking involved, nor is any special equipment such as boots or country clothing required.

Although the Lake District is understandably the most popular part of Cumbria, and its towns and villages form a good proportion of the contents of this book, there are many settlements in the remainder of the county which are less familiar to visitors but have a lot to offer and should not be neglected. They also have the considerable advantage of being far less crowded during the holiday season.

As it is expected that private motor vehicles will, often of necessity, be used to reach the towns and villages, appropriate parking places are suggested. Should there be an operational railway station or a useful bus service, this can be regarded as a desirable alternative and may, indeed, be combined with one or more of the trails to make a varied excursion. Appleby, Ravenglass, Ulverston, and Maryport all come readily to mind as offering a combination of rail and trail. With regard to bus and trail, the popular centres in the Lake District all have reasonably good services, particularly those on the 555/556 route of Cumberland Motor Services. Timetables are available at Tourist Information Centres.

For the type of excursion envisaged, refreshments are often important, adding yet another element to the enjoyment of visiting a town or village. The well-earned cup of tea or coffee, or perhaps something stronger, is an entirely pleasant adjunct to relaxation and to observing local life. Most of the towns and villages included offer a selection of inns and/or teashops which will be self-evident as a trail is followed, and need no mention. In the few places which are less well provided for, the availability or otherwise of refreshments is indicated.

Norman Buckley

Contents

Locations of Trails

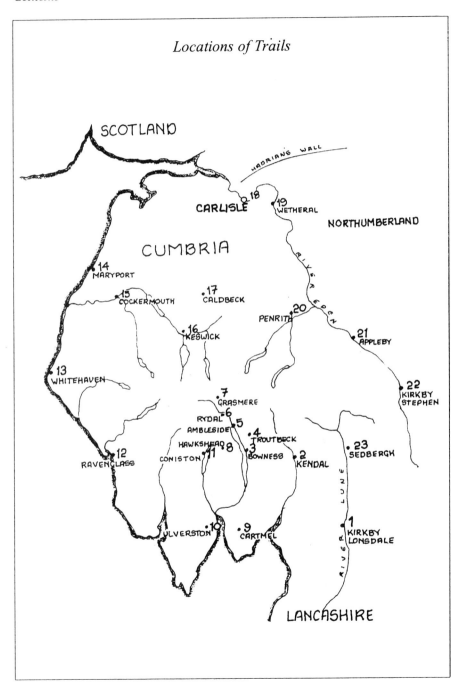

Introduction

Cumbria

The modern county of Cumbria was newly formed in 1974 by the amalgamation of the old counties of Cumberland and Westmorland with the Furness district of Lancashire and a small part of Yorkshire. In geographical and administrative terms this appeared to be quite logical, but many local people and organisations still cling to the old county names, showing deep loyalties which have prevailed over the ensuing years. Cumbria has survived recent attempts at dismemberment.

In considering Cumbria as a holiday or leisure destination, most visitors will naturally focus on the Lake District, the undisputed jewel in the county's crown, Britain's biggest and finest National Park, an area in which mountain, lake, and woodland are wonderfully blended to provide outstanding scenery throughout its compact area. The inevitable price to be paid for this beauty is its huge popularity as a visitor area, with the consequent and constant pressure, both for unsuitable and damaging developments and on the roads and facilities of the more accessible towns and villages during the greater part of the year.

But Cumbria is much more than just the Lake District. To the south, Furness has the north shore of Morecambe Bay and the rolling countryside which was once largely the preserve of the all-powerful Furness Abbey, with farming and the early exploitation of the mineral resources, served by small ports along the coast. Nineteenth century industrialisation brought the rapid growth of Barrow in Furness as a great shipbuilding and iron and steel centre, while further to the east

Grange over Sands was established as a select residential area, with aspirations as a dignified seaside holiday resort.

North of Barrow, the Cumberland coastline and the strip of land separating mountains and sea, is generally bleak and is suffering from the dereliction of the once dominant coal and iron industries, but it is by no means without character. Ravenglass, Whitehaven, and Maryport are among the towns and villages which are of historic interest, while the British Nuclear Fuels plant at Sellafield is proving to be one of the most popular visitor attractions in the region. Even futher north, the marshy Solway coastal area has fine views across to the hills of southern Scotland.

Carlisle is steeped in history as a border stronghold and is the gateway to sections of Hadrian's wall and the remote part of the county between the Wall and the Scottish border.

Most of the east of Cumbria is occupied by two fine river valleys, the Eden flowing north to the Solway Firth, and the Lune flowing south to Lancaster and Morecambe Bay. The Eden valley is noted for a whole string of attractive villages, and the Lune has its gorge, providing a through route for north/south transport, at least since Roman times. Virtually the whole of the eastern flank is along the high Pennines, including Cross Fell, the highest point. Coupled with the Lake District summits, this gives Cumbria a clean sweep of England's highest mountains.

Cumbria is a county of rich diversity and strong character, with the older towns and villages much affected by successive invasions and incursions from the time of the Romans onwards, and their vernacular architecture blending harmoniously with the natural environment. The climate has also played its part in shaping the landscape and, arguably, the people. The notorious rainfall of the Lake District is essential in preserving the green freshness and the sparkling quality of light which contributes so much to the unique charm, and also in satisfying the thirst of Manchester for good quality water, while the wind off the Irish Sea ensures that the Cumberland coast will never become an "English Riviera". Coupled with the predominance of high pastures and meagre soil over much of the county, this hard climate has dictated a high proportion of sheep farming and a scarcity of the more profitable arable cultivation which dominates the softer south of the country.

Tourism has long been a very important part of the local economy and is officially encouraged; those visitors who are prepared to leave their vehicles and to take just a little trouble to explore some of the less familiar attractions of this most magnificent of counties will be richly rewarded.

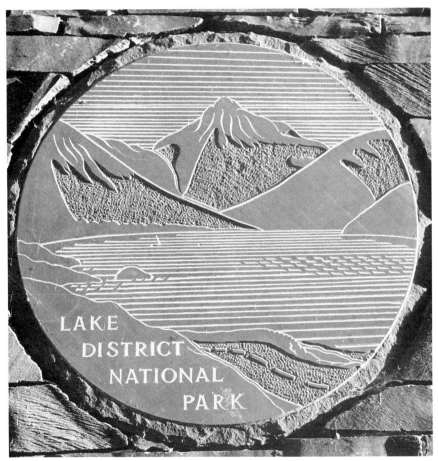

National Park plaque:spot it on Trail 3 (Bowness)

1. Kirkby Lonsdale

Description

Compared with Keswick or Bowness, Kirkby Lonsdale is not a holiday town, but it is increasingly having to come to terms with considerable numbers of visitors. However, in essence it remains as it has been for a very long time – a "real" little town of solid grey stone with business-like shops along the narrow streets, some of which have intriguing names like "Salt Pie Lane", "Horse Mark", and "Jingling Lane". There are plenty of old inns and a good Market Place with a generous "cross" erected in 1905. The original market charter was granted in 1227.

The area was well known to the Romans, who had a fort (*Calacum*) two miles to the south, where the Leck Beck joins the River Lune. Centuries later, in 1745, the Young Pretender passed by on his ill-fated attempt to restore the House of Stuart to the throne.

The Trail

Half a mile to the south of the town centre the A65 crosses the River Lune by a modern bridge. Close by is the superseded "Devil's Bridge", with substantial car parking on the approach roads on each side of the bridge. This is the recommended start to the trail.

¤   The celebrated "Devil's Bridge" is of great antiquity, claimed by some to be of Roman origin. It is more likely to be medieval;

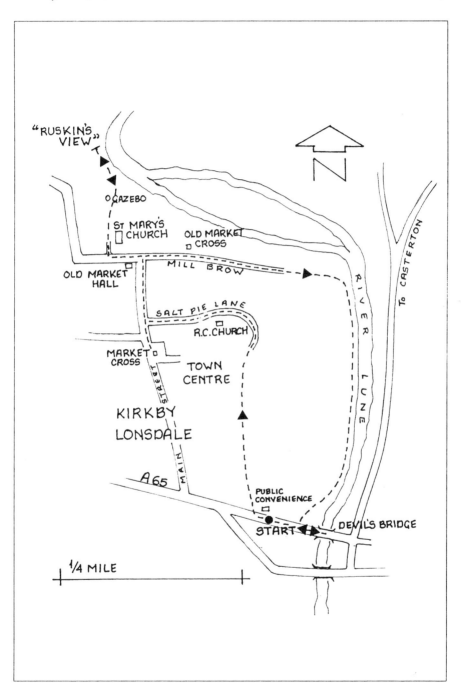

repairs were carried out six hundred years ago and, until the present road bridge was constructed, it carried all the through traffic across the Lune. The three arches rise gracefully high over the water, attracting the attention of the great landscape painter J.M.W. Turner during one of his northern tours between 1816 and 1818. The name results from a legend: "an old woman needed to cross the river, but the water was in flood and it was impossible for her to wade across as she normally did. The devil appeared and offered to build a bridge, on condition that he could claim the soul of the first creature to cross, expecting, of course, that the woman would go straight across. But she was too crafty for him, throwing a bun for her dog which then dashed across and duly lost its soul to the devil".

¤   The immediate surroundings of the bridge are also very attractive and are open to the public for picnics and general recreational use, although swimming in the fine rock pools is apparently discouraged.

Kirkby Lonsdale church

¤ From the bridge walk past the public conveniences and turn right to follow a signposted footpath, surfaced and tree-lined, towards the centre of Kirkby Lonsdale. As the path forks and becomes a minor roadway, keep right, passing the Roman Catholic Church of St Joseph. Turn sharp left, then right, into Salt Pie Lane, soon reaching Main Street.

¤ The Market Place, with its substantial "cross", is to the left; the Tourist Information Centre is a little further along Main Street. From the Market Place, return along Main Street. As the road bends, becoming Market Street, on the corner is the former Market Hall of 1854. The upper floors were used as a Magistrates' Court and, later, a cinema. Although the building has been converted into shops, the original iron gates are still in place.

¤ From Market Street, turn right into Church Street, with pleasant stone houses leading to the impressive church gates. As the church is approached, there is a replica of an 18th century sundial on the left. Although St Mary's Church has been much restored,

"Ruskin's View"

the base of the tower, with a well-carved doorway, is Norman, as are some internal features. The font is very old indeed. In 1818, Turner produced a watercolour of this churchyard.

¤ From the church continue to the old little raised gazebo and follow the signposted footpath to "Ruskin's View 100 yards". The broad, richly green swathe of the river and its valley, backed by the wild Pennine hills which form the eastern boundary of Cumbria was much admired by John Ruskin and, like Friar's Crag on Derwentwater, has become formalised as a "Ruskin" viewpoint.

¤ Return to Market Street, turn left, and then fork left down Mill Brow. On the left is the original market cross, now relegated to obscurity. Go over a stile into a nature site and turn right to follow the easy and very pleasant footpath which returns alongside the river to Devil's Bridge.

---

2. Kendal

Description

Largest town of the old Westmorland county, and centre for an extensive rural hinterland, Kendal is a busy, bustling place, particularly when its own quite modest population is enhanced by shoppers from the villages and/or by holiday visitors. Long regarded as the "gateway to the lakes", the town has, happily, been by-passed for many years by the M6 and by the main road linking Windermere to the motorway. The sombre appearance of the town, with much use of limestone as a building material, has resulted in the nickname of "the auld grey town".

The earliest castle was sited to the west of the river and the present main street; it was replaced by a more imposing stone structure, now itself a ruin, on a mound to the east of the river. In later centuries a maze of alleyways and courtyards was a highly characteristic feature of the town centre until 20th century clearance took its toll. The claim that the form of this development, in particular the narrow entrances, was for defensive purposes is quite wrong, as the Scottish raids had ceased many centuries previously. It had much more to do with cramming the largest possible number of people on the smallest possible area of land.

Long a centre of the woollen industry, one local product was the cloth called "Kendal Green", mentioned in Shakespeare. Nowadays, shoes and insurance are prominent.

Finding places on the main street can be confusing, as that same thoroughfare has three names; from the north – Stricklandgate, then Highgate, followed by Kirkland. Despite the traffic and the much criticised one way system, Kendal is still quite a pleasant place to shop, particularly away from the main street. Pedestrianisation has improved Finkle Street and the market area (open air market on Wednesdays and Saturdays), whilst the adjacent Westmorland Centre is a good example of the smaller type of modern shopping complex.

The railway station, to the north of the town centre and allowed to become very run down over the years, is served only by the Windermere branch line trains, although there are now through workings to Manchester and its airport. Oxenholme station, two miles from the town centre, has a reasonably good service on the west coast main line.

The Trail

In a fair sized town with such historic interest, a fully comprehensive trail would occupy many hours. The present trail aims to include the most significant features within a more modest compass, but will require more time and effort than the great majority in the book. To appreciate the rich complexity of the town architecture, along the main streets it is essential to look at the first and higher floors as so very few of the shop fronts in any way do justice to the buildings of which they are, inevitably, the most obvious part.

¤   Start at the unmistakable (and rather controversial) modern pagoda at the junction of Finkle Street and Stricklandgate. Proceed down Finkle Street. In a short distance, on the left, is the entrance to the New Shambles, formerly occupied by butchers' shops. A civic society plaque gives a short history of the Shambles. It was obviously not a place to linger in the good old days! At the far end of the Shambles the Market Place is reached, with the entrance to the Westmorland Centre opposite.

¤   Turn right to descend Branthwaite Brow. On the right are buildings with a curious front wall construction – prefabricated iron plating, resulting from street widening in 1851. The last building

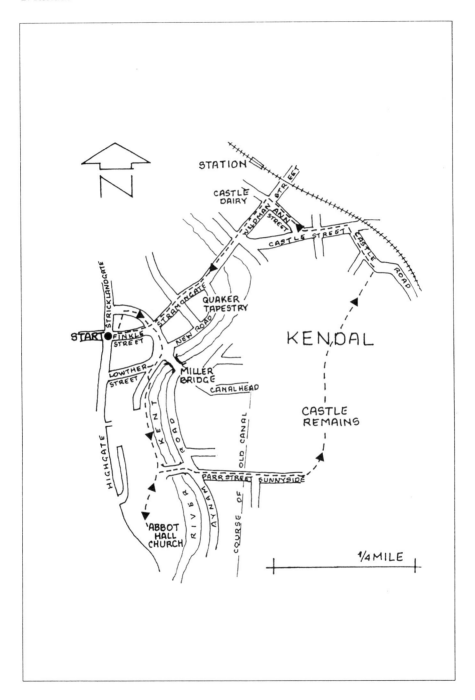

The Shambles

on the left, the "Chocolate House", is one of Kendal's oldest. Continue across the junction, descending towards the River Kent, but turn right, then right again into Lowther Street. A few yards up the street is a snuff factory, another traditional Kendal trade, with the figure of a Turk holding a roll of tobacco, high on the wall.

¤ Return to the river and turn right along the Waterside footpath. Look back to Miller bridge which, in 1818 replaced an old bridge giving access to a corn mill. A monument to James Cropper, a former Mayor and well known local manufacturer of paper, is soon reached. Turn right, across the public gardens, and then left to reach the elegant Georgian House, Abbot Hall, home of a small but renowned art gallery. Adjacent is the Museum of Lakeland Life and Industry (joint entrance tickets are available).

¤   From the Abbot Hall, turn left again to the parish church of the Holy Trinity. Of unusual width, and with an 80ft. tower, this fine building originated early in the 13th century but has since been much modified. It is open daily to 4.30pm in the summer months and most mornings during winter. Inside, there is much of interest, with memorials of the Parr and Strickland families. More modern is the "family of man" sculpture by Josefina de Vasconcellos (see Rydal, page 35).

¤   Return to the Cropper memorial by the river and cross Jennings Bridge. Turn right, cross Aynam Road, and turn left into Parr Street, named after Katherine Parr, Henry VIII's sixth and final wife, who was fortunate enough to outlive him. Kendal Castle was the home of Katherine's grandfather and there is a dubious claim that she was born here. Part way up the street is a bridge over the former Kendal and Lancaster Canal, opened in 1819 to provide cheap transport for bulk goods, particularly coal from Lancashire, hastening the transition to steam power for local industry. The terminus of the canal was a little way to the north at Canal Head, close to Miller Bridge. As the railway came to Kendal in 1846, the importance of the canal soon declined, but it did continue as a navigable waterway until the time of World War II. This section is now drained and filled and serves as a cycle track. The bridge can be examined by descending to the right.

¤   Continue into Sunnyside, go through the gate at the top, and climb the steep little knoll on which the castle stands. This was Kendal's second castle, replacing a motte and bailey structure on the other side of the town, probably late in the 12th century. Most of the substantial stone buildings were erected between 1220 and 1280, but by the 16th century the castle was derelict.

¤   From the castle entrance follow the broad track heading north to Castle Road. Turn left then left again at Castle Street, right into Ann Street and left into Wildman Street. On the right is the oldest occupied house in Kendal, Castle Dairy. The name is almost certainly a corruption of Castle Dowry, as the house is believed to have been given by Sir Thomas Parr to his daughter Agnes as part of her dowry when she married Sir Thomas Strickland in about 1455. The architectural features include a chimney stack which would look more at home in Troutbeck than amongst the bustle of present-day Kendal.

Castle Dairy

¤ Continue over Stramongate Bridge, widened in 1793, but with an earlier bridge visible from underneath. Cross New Road to the Friends Meeting House. This is a very old Quaker site. Following a visit by George Fox in 1652, the first meeting house was built here in 1688, with the addition of a school a few years later. The present building, designed to accommodate 850 people, was erected in 1815/16. It is now home to the Quaker Tapestry Exhibition. Interpretation of the tapestry is facilitated by the use of personal headphones and a video display. The exhibition is open from 10am to 5pm on Mondays to Saturdays from April to late autumn.

¤ Continue along Stramongate, then Finkle Street, to return to the pagoda.

3. Bowness

Description

B owness is the true holiday portion of the Windermere/Bowness built-up area. It is an immensely popular resort, particularly for day visitors, and in high season it is a very busy place indeed, when the promenade, gift shops, inns and cafes, are bustling with activity. However, the core of Bowness is a very old former lakeside boating and fishing community, with some buildings dating from the 17th century.

This trail explores both the historic and the present-day attractions of the village.

The Trail

S tart at the Bowness Tourist Information Centre, well-situated by the junction of Glebe Road and the promenade. Included in the centre is the Countryside Theatre, which has a comprehensive programme of talks on subjects of local interest throughout the season; the centre is also the starting point for guided walks. Behind the centre are public tennis courts, putting green and a large pitch and putt course.

¤ Proceed along the promenade, which is the calling point for the lake "steamer" services. There are also many and varied lake excursions, with motor boats and rowing boats for hire. At the far

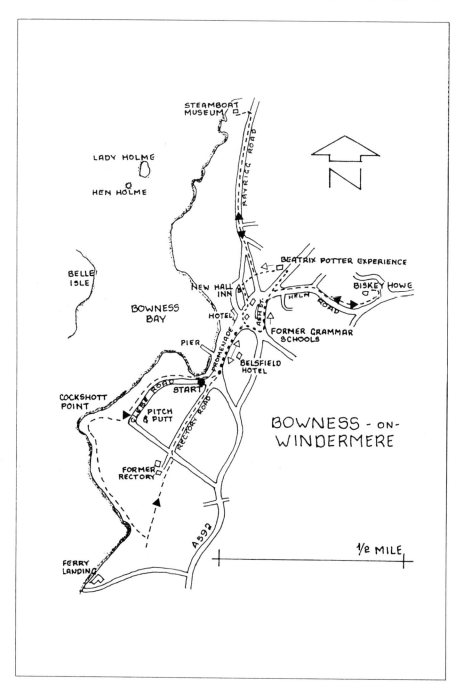

end of the promenade are the locally well-known boatmen's "cushion huts", now refurbished but originally dating from around the turn of the century, when Bowness Bay was at its peak as a tourist boating centre.

Lake "steamer" at Bowness

¤ Above, to the right, is the imposing Belsfield Hotel, built as a lakeside mansion for Baroness de Sternberg in 1845 and purchased in 1869 by H.W. Schneider, the famous Barrow in Furness-based industrialist. Schneider frequently "commuted" to his office in Barrow, using his steam launch "Esperance" from Bowness to Lakeside, then a Furness Railway train with a special private coach on to Barrow. A familiar sight was Schneider's butler walking down from the house to the jetty carrying a silver salver with the great man's breakfast, to be eaten on the launch. The doorway in the boundary wall can still be seen. When the house later became a hotel, an extra storey was added to the building.

¤ Keep to the main street, turning right into the Kendal Road. Brantfell Road rises steeply to the right of Laurel Cottage, a 17th century building which was the first Bowness Grammar School. Just above is the building, now divided into apartments, which was the second Bowness Grammar School. Look at the plaque on the front wall to find the name of the celebrity involved in the stone laying ceremony.

¤   Return along the pedestrianised Ash Street, with its attractive jumble of shops and cafes, to the main road, now the bottom of Crag Brow. Yet more shops line both sides for a considerable distance up the hill. Unless you would like to extend the walk, (see option 1, below) go up only as far as the "Beatrix Potter Experience", situated on the left down a steep little slope.

¤   The Beatrix Potter building, described below, is on two levels; exit to Rayrigg Road, past the cafe on the lower level (for the Steamboat Museum, see 2, below). Across Rayrigg Road is the area of tight knit little streets which was the original village. Perhaps the most interesting building is the New Hall Inn, now known as The Hole in t'Wall, visited by Dickens. Thomas Long-mire, champion wrestler of all England was landlord here from 1852 to 1860.

¤   Head for St Mary's parish Church, a solid low building restored in 1483, which provides an oasis of calm at the heart of the holiday bustle of modern Bowness. If the church is open have a look at the wooden statue of the patron saint, and the fine old glass in the east window, allegedly salvaged from Cartmel Priory at the time of the Dissolution. Nineteenth century restoration has produced a light, not unattractive, church interior.

¤   Return along the main street to the promenade and Information Centre (for the final suggested extension, see 3 below).

Extensions

1. For the first possible extension to the trail, turn right from the main road (Crag Brow) into Helm Road and climb quite steeply past the Windermere Hydro Hotel. After the hotel, the mound on the left is Biskey Howe, which can be reached by taking an angled footpath or, more easily, by continuing up the road and turning sharp left along

a very obvious track at the top. From this upper side of the knoll there is also a wheelchair track to the viewpoint, which is very attractive, with mini rock faces and superb views over the lake, to Claiffe Heights and beyond.

2. For the second extension, walk along Rayrigg Road for a quarter of a mile or so to the Steamboat Museum, described below.

3. The third suggested extension is to walk along Glebe Road, passing the traditional pavilion on the left, and with the modern boating and shopping facilities between the road and the lake on the right. The views along the lake to the mountains are wonderful, with the Fairfield Horseshoe prominent. As Glebe Road bends to the left, carry straight on along a good footpath signposted to Cockshott Point, which is a very short distance ahead. From this pleasant promontory Belle Isle, with what is claimed to be the first truly circular house in Britain, is seen at close range. Return either by the same route, or complete a circuit by continuing along the footpath to the left, then turning left at a junction of footpaths, back to Glebe Road. Cross the road and follow Rectory Road by the side of the cemetery back to the Information Centre.

Beatrix Potter Experience

The Beatrix Potter Experience has been created in an old laundry building. The series of tableaux of larger than life characters from the much loved children's books, coupled with audio-visual presentations and shop, is a great family attraction, open daily throughout the year. Also within the same building is a modern theatre, inspired by, and with links to, Alan Ayckbourn's theatre at Scarborough, and a cafeteria serving good light refreshments.

Steamboat Museum

Created on the site of a sand and gravel extraction plant, this modern museum houses many of the beautiful steamboats which were an important feature of elegant late Victorian and Edwardian life in the district. Other exhibits include early examples of both speed boats and sailing craft. In season there are steamboat trips on the lake; light refreshments and a picnic area are available.

4. Troutbeck

Description

S trung out along the western side of the valley, at the level where springs have always provided a reliable supply of water, Troutbeck is not so much a geographically cohesive village as a series of linked hamlets, with the parish church situated by the side of the Trout Beck, some distance below. Much of what is now visible dates from the mid to late 17th century, when good prices for wool enhanced the prosperity of the farming community. Troutbeck has probably changed less in the ensuing 300 years than almost any other Lakeland settlement, and the succession of buildings seen along this trail encompasses almost every facet of local traditional construction.

Quarrying in the 18th century also brought some prosperity and the arrival of the railway at Windermere in 1847 did bring tourism, with some new merchants' houses and the rebuilding of two inns. Nevertheless, the village was still generally regarded as poor, dirty, and neglected when compared with Windermere or Ambleside.

Scenically, the setting is fine, facing the long Yoke, Ill Bell, Froswick ridge across a broad valley, with the bulk of Wansfell providing shelter from the worst of westerly weather.

Fortunately, the main A592 road keeps closer to the valley bottom, by-passing the great majority of the village. To the north and east the large Troutbeck Park Farm, owned and lived in for many years by Beatrix Potter and the scene of many of the illustrations in her book "The Fairy Caravan", occupies the valley. Like so many other properties owned by Beatrix Potter, the farm was left to the National Trust.

[For a detailed description of a large selection of the old buildings in

Troutbeck, the book "Vernacular Architecture of the Lake Counties" – R.W. Brunskill – Faber paperbacks, is recommended].

Troutbeck

The Trail

The main A592 road runs from Windermere to Ullswater via the Kirkstone Pass. Just short of Troutbeck Church, turn left into a lane which leads upwards to Troutbeck village. On the left, by the beck, is informal parking space for several cars.

¤   Ascend the lane to reach the village by the post office/stores. At the top of the hill are Low Fold and the Spinnery. The former has a projecting oriel window at first floor level, whilst the latter has a good example of the Lakeland "spinning gallery" on the side.

¤   Turn left towards Townend. Below, on the left, are Low House, with fine corbelled chimney stack, and another very old house which was derelict a few years ago and is gradually being restored. At the next road junction Town End is reached. Across the road from the house is a bank barn still in agricultural use. The canopy over the barn doors is extended to form a gallery. Look for the initials G. & E.B. and the date 1666 over a window, and the extension on the north of this building where part of a former cruck frame has been re-used as a door lintel.

¤   Townend is a fine example of a "statesman's" (yeoman farmer) house built about 1626, with later alterations. It was occupied by the Browne family from that date until 1943. Inside are carved woodwork, papers, old furniture and domestic implements used and collected by the family over the centuries. It is now owned by the National Trust and is open to the public from April to October. A visit to Townend is virtually essential to under-standing and appreciating Troutbeck both as a historic and a living village.

¤   To see a more modern minor curiosity, walk 100 yards down the road opposite, where a traditional AA. sign is still in situ on the end of a building. In pre-motorway days, London was a (slow!) 271 mile journey from Troutbeck. Town Foot, Town End House, and Town End Farm are all basically 17th century buildings. Return to the road junction and to the post office/stores, where

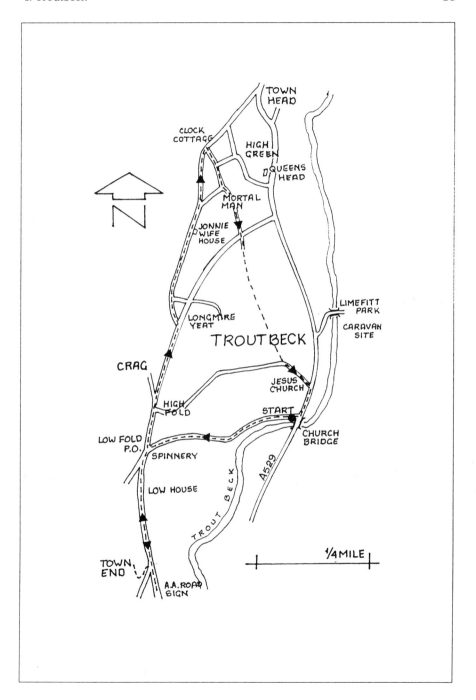

an old sign displays the availability of cups of tea and coffee, and continue along the main street.

¤   The next hamlet is High Fold, another attractive cluster of buildings, with an unusual walled green. High up the bank to the left is a remarkable renovation of a long derelict house. The first of Troutbeck's "wells", that dedicated to St John, is reached, soon followed by St James's.

¤   Before reaching the hamlet of Longmire Yeat, there is a gap in the buildings giving the opportunity for long views across the valley to the fine ridge which includes the summits of Yoke, Ill Bell, and Froswick as it rises towards the summit of High Street, crossed by the well-known Roman road of the same name.

¤   After Longmire Yeat comes St Margaret's Well and a long stone barn opposite. Unusually, this barn has both a hipped roof and a chimney stack. A King Edward VII post box is set in the wall of a 19th century house close by and, just before the "Mortal Man" Inn, is "Jonnie Wife House", a range of buildings including a house, a barn, and a former granary, all at right angles to the slope.

¤   The "Mortal Man" was established in 1689, roughly contemporary with so much of Troutbeck, but was rebuilt and greatly enlarged late in the 19th century. The Inn sign, originally painted by the celebrated local artist Julius Caesar Ibbotson, who lived in the village from 1802 to 1805 (the present sign is a copy), with its cautionary verse, is a widely appreciated local curiosity.

¤   Continue along the road as far as the obviously named Clock Cottage, and turn right into a bridleway. Keep right at a fork and descend through High Green hamlet towards the "Mortal Man". The large, well-built barn on the right, with continuous canopy, is late 19th century. Bear left before the "Mortal Man" along a rough surfaced lane and head for the church, going straight across at a junction of paths. One section of this path may be muddy in wet weather. Turn left as a lane is reached or, alternatively, go directly through the graveyard to the church, dedicated, unusually, to Jesus.

¤   The date over the door is 1736, when it was last rebuilt, but inside are ancient beams in the roof and much 16th and early 17th century woodwork, including the parish chest and table by the font. The chancel stalls were brought from the old Calgarth Hall, beside Windermere. Perhaps most famous is the east window, where the stained glass is the work of the pre-Raphaelite artist Burne-Jones, probably with assistance from his friends William Morris and Ford Maddox Brown. The Royal Arms above the gallery door were painted in 1737.

¤   A few yards further along the main road is the right turn to the car park.

Troutbeck, with mountains beyond

5. Ambleside

Description

Is Ambleside a town, or is it merely a village? The guide books are uniformly agreed; Ambleside is a town. Nevertheless, those who live there resolutely refer to it as "the village". It doesn't, of course, really matter; what is undisputable is that Ambleside is deservedly a very popular place indeed, situated close to the heart of Lakeland, just one mile north of the tip of Windermere. The strategic position has long been of importance for communications. Today's hordes are directly in a line of succession of travellers which started with the Romans.

Despite being almost overwhelmed by visitors, and particularly by their motor vehicles, for much of the year, there is still a strong core of community, most evident in the winter, and by no means all the shops are aimed solely at the tourists.

Although there are some unfortunate modern aberrations the diversified buildings still form an attractive whole, strongly Victorian in the centre, but much older on the rising ground to the north-east. Hills and mountains on three sides provide both a perfect setting and viewpoints from which the town can be admired. At the edge of Windermere, Waterhead was once a separate community but is now regarded as an outlying part of Ambleside.

The Trail

The large pay and display car park at Waterhead, with information centre and public conveniences, is well-sited for those approaching from the south, avoiding involvement with the Ambleside town traffic.

¤   Cross the road to admire the wonderful view down the lake. To the left is the Victorian pier from which the scheduled service of lake "steamers" operates. Varied cruises and hire boats are also available close by. Turn right to walk along Borrans Road, passing the Wateredge and Regent Hotels. Turn left at a gate just after the Wateredge Hotel and descend a ramp into Borrans Park, equipped with seats and picnic tables. Follow the surfaced path, suitable for wheelchairs and pushchairs, towards the lake shore, soon bending to the right.

Waterhead, Ambleside

¤   A gate in the wall on the left leads to the Roman fort of Galava. Here, the first fort was constructed in 79 A.D. to safeguard the route from Brougham to Ravenglass, via the Hardknott Pass. Following problems with flooding of the low-lying site, the whole area was raised and a second fort was constructed in about 122

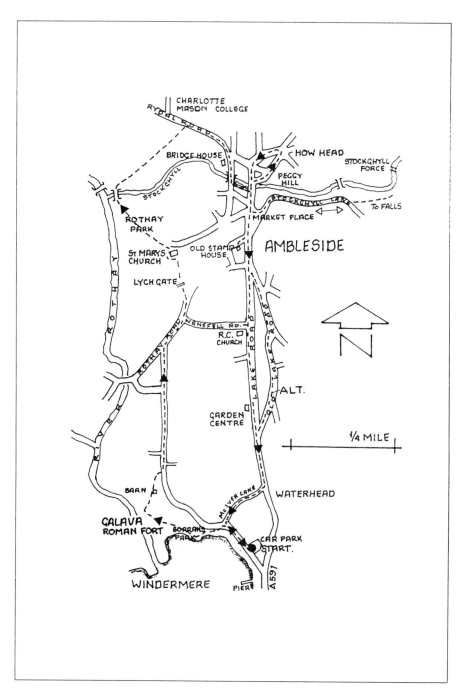

A.D. Although excavations have been carried out, there isn't a great deal to see on the ground, but recent assumption of direct management by the site owners, the National Trust, may well result in much more of interest being made available for visitors. The adjacent rocky knoll is a good viewpoint.

¤ From the fort turn right to head across the grass towards the prominent dated bank barn, also in National Trust ownership. Rejoin Borrans Road at a farm gate, taking care with the traffic on this busy roadway. With a wheelchair or pram, a return to Borrans Road via the park is advisable, as the grassy area by the barn is often muddy.

¤ Continue along Borrans Road. Ahead, Fairfield and its outlying mountains form a fine backdrop to the high steepled parish church, while to the left, the modest height of Loughrigg is close, more intimate and friendly. After passing the Rothay Manor Hotel, the road bends to the right; look out for a Victorian horse drinking trough on the left of the road, inscribed "Ho everyone that thirsteth".

¤ Turn left into a broad, unsurfaced, roadway leading to an outlying lych gate erected in 1977 to commemorate the Queen's Silver Jubilee, and carry on through the burial ground to St Mary's parish church. To the right is a recreation area with tennis, bowls and pitch and putt. At the far end of the burial ground climb the steep little bank to the church (the bank can be avoided by turning right at a pathway which leads round the east end of the church)

¤ Designed by the apparently ubiquitous Sir Gilbert Scott, St Mary's is spacious and dignified, but rather bland inside. However, of particular interest are, firstly, a large mural painted by Gordon Ransom in 1944, depicting the traditional annual rushbearing ceremony and, secondly, a virgin and child statue by the celebrated local sculptress, Josefina de Vasconcellos, also mentioned in other trails in this book, particularly Rydal.

¤ Leave the church and turn sharp left along the cul de sac roadway into Rothay Park, with picnic area, children's play area and public conveniences. Head across the park towards the R. Rothay, cross

Stock Beck on a flat bridge, but don't cross the main river. Take the second footpath on the right, which has a wheelchair symbol on its signpost. The path is bounded by upright slates, much more common in the Hawkshead area. As the main Rydal Road is reached, Charlotte Mason College is opposite with a fine colonial style building, formerly a private house, as its core.

¤   Turn right towards Bridge House, Ambleside's best-known building, spanning Stock Beck. Despite suggestions that it originated as an ingenious way of avoiding payment of some form of land taxation, the truth about this house over the water is unfortunately more prosaic; it was merely the apple store in the orchard of the former Ambleside Manor. Cross the road and stand on the bridge over Stock Beck. Upstream was Ambleside's industrial zone; an array of water powered mills, grinding corn, making bobbins, and fulling cloth as the need and the trade ebbed and flowed over the centuries. In a further 25 yards, turn left into Rattle Gill, an intriguing footway leading to North Road; one water-wheel may be seen on the side of the former mill across the beck.

¤   Cross North Road and ascend Penny Hill. All around is old Ambleside, some of it very old indeed. Join Fairview Road and follow round to the left, towards the redundant St Anne's Church, now converted into apartments. Bear left around one of Ambleside's oldest buildings, How Head, which may, in part, be as early as the 15th century. Now divided into different occupancies, including the oddly-named Dwarf Hall, this building has many of the typical Lakeland constructional features. Continue down Chapel Hill, turn left into North Road, and join the main street opposite the Queens Hotel. Straight ahead is the old market building, to the left is the Salutation, a former coaching inn.

¤   [Should time and inclination permit an extension to the trail, turn left and then left again at a signpost "The Waterfalls ½ mile" and follow Stock Gill Lane. The fall has been a popular excursion since Victorian times and may be visited without any problems of muddy or difficult paths but, inevitably, there is quite an uphill pull].

¤ Carry on through the former Market Place. A diversion of a few yards into Church Street will reveal the Old Stamp House, where a plaque records William Wordsworth's tenure of the office of Distributor of Stamps for Westmorland from 1813 to 1843. In reality, Wordsworth generally kept his stamps and money at his house in Rydal and made little use of this office. If the noise of the traffic along Lake Road is a nuisance, a left fork into Old Lake Road does provide a quieter route, but there is no footway and the Roman Catholic church is by-passed.

¤ If the main road is followed, half way down Wansfell Road is found the modern Roman Catholic church of Mater Amabilis, with a much admired interior. The two routes come together opposite Hayes Garden Centre, now a major all-weather tourist attraction. Adjacent is a wooden building, imported from Norway and erected as a studio in 1911 by Alfred Heaton Cooper, father of William Heaton Cooper of Grasmere studio, who died in 1995 at a ripe old age. Opposite the garden centre is the unassuming headquarters of Lakeland's busiest mountain rescue team.

¤ After passing the garden centre turn right at a bus stop into the unsignposted McIver Lane, soon reaching Borrans Road and turning left back to the starting point.

Landing stage at Waterhead

6. Rydal

Description

Merely a hamlet squeezed between the steep slopes of Nab Scar and the tranquil beauty of the privately owned Rydal Water, Rydal (Rye Dale – the valley where rye is grown) would hardly qualify for the inclusion of a village trail were it not for two important factors. Firstly, for the last thirty seven years of his life Rydal Mount was the home of William Wordsworth; secondly, the grounds of historic Rydal Hall, containing much of interest, are to some extent accessible to the public.

The Trail

By road from either Ambleside or Grasmere turn into the cul de sac roadway which rises from the main road to Rydal Mount, the church, and Rydal Hall. Start the trail at St Mary's Church, formerly known as Rydal Chapel, which was built on her orchard by Lady le Fleming of Rydal Hall in 1823, at a cost of £1500. Externally the squat building is pleasant enough but is unremarkable. Wordsworth, who became a chapel warden here, wrote a poem in its praise, but did consider it to be rather cramped. It was enlarged in 1884, many years after his death.

¤   Inside the church, the Wordsworth pew is at the front, on the left, while across the aisle is the pew which was occupied by Dr.

Arnold and his family. The well-known headmaster of Rugby school built the house "Fox How" across the valley at Under Loughrigg in 1833, allowing his friend Wordsworth to exert great influence on the design. Later, the house passed into the hands of Dr. Arnold's son Matthew, who spent many holidays there. The le Fleming family separated themselves from the rest of the congregation by occupying the balcony at the rear of the church, which has its own external entrance. There are several commemoration plaques and windows relating to members of these families.

Rydal church interior

¤ Behind the church is Dora's field, purchased by Wordsworth in 1826 when, as a mere tenant, he feared eviction from Rydal Mount by his landlord, Lady Diana le Fleming. He commissioned plans for the erection of his own house on the field but, on a change of mind by Lady le Fleming, the plans were abandoned and the field later given to his daughter Dora. The field, which is now owned by the National Trust, is noted for its bank of daffodils, but it is certainly not the subject of the famous poem!

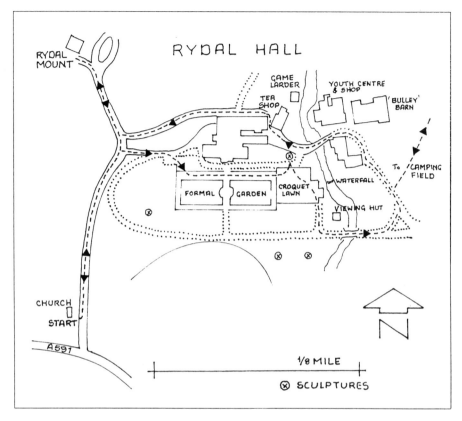

RYDAL HALL

RYDAL MOUNT

GAME LARDER

YOUTH CENTRE & SHOP

TEA SHOP

'BULLEY' BARN

To CAMPING FIELD

WATERFALL

FORMAL GARDEN

CROQUET LAWN

VIEWING HUT

CHURCH

START

A591

N

⅛ MILE

⊗ SCULPTURES

¤ Return to the road and walk up to Rydal Mount, at the top, on the left. Standing in several acres of attractive gardens, this comparatively grand house is an 18th century enlargement of a much earlier farmhouse. The fine views from the house include Windermere and Loughrigg Fell, across the valley. It was home to the Wordsworths for thirty seven years after they left Grasmere. Accepting that after 1813 the great man's youthful fervour had faded, and with it had also gone most of his finest work, a visit to Rydal Mount is still of absorbing interest. Here, Wordsworth's fame grew; honours, including that of Poet Laureate, were awarded, and he was visited by the great literary figures of the day, including many Americans as his fame spread across the Atlantic Ocean. With the exception of three weeks in mid-winter and winter Tuesdays, the house is open to the public throughout the year and remains furnished much as it was in Wordsworth's day. There are chair seats embroidered by Mary and Dorothy Wordsworth and by Sara Hutchinson; family portraits adorn the walls. The garden is delightful, with terraces made by Wordsworth himself, where he, and others such as the tragically unfulfilled Hartley Coleridge, would pace up and down, either seeking inspiration or perhaps just ameliorating the effects of a heavy meal. Above the house a well-used bridleway, the former "coffin road", leads towards Grasmere. With Dove Cottage at one end and Rydal Mount at the other, it is hardly surprising that this track was a favourite ramble for the Wordsworths.

¤ Continue the trail by crossing the road and descending a little to the lower of the two entrances to Rydal Hall grounds. The gardens, but not the Hall itself, are open to the public and there is a right of way which goes across

¤ Rydal Park towards Ambleside. The Hall was the seat of the le Flemings, one of Lakeland's comparatively few grand families, for more than 300 years, prior to its lease in 1963, and subsequent purchase, by the Diocese of Carlisle. The Hall is now used as a conference centre and retreat, with a camp-site and youth centre in the grounds. Head for a small wooden gate on the right which gives access to the formal gardens at the front of the Hall. Before reaching the gate, however, look down the slope to the right, where a block of stone has been most ingeniously carved by students working with Josefina de Vasconcellos. Resident in Ambleside, nonagenarian Josefina has a considerable and well-earned reputation as an artist of strong views and great talent. Cartmel Priory houses one of her best known creations.

¤ Continue through the formal gardens, passing a fountain. In visiting Rydal Hall, please remember that the Hall is occupied by a small Christian community and that peace and quiet are an important adjunct to community life. Although the gardens were set in a landscape largely determined by the 18th century, they took their present form early in the 20th century, under Thomas Mawson, who had international fame as a landscape gardener. From the front terrace the Hall itself may be admired. The well-proportioned façade is a late 18th century addition to a largely 17th century building, originally of more modest size and appearance. Even earlier, the first Rydal Hall was situated at the far side of the main road, more than ½ mile distant from the present building. What a pity that the stonework of the Hall is cement rendered!

¤ Above the croquet lawn at the far end of the gardens is a fine example of Josefina's work, a more than life-sized figure of Christ, which some viewers find quite disturbing.

¤ Leave the gardens by a descending flight of steps in the corner by the croquet lawn and turn left to the bridge over Rydal Beck. Across the trackway and before the bridge is the Garden of Meditation, with its three pools and only the ever present sound of the rushing beck normally intruding on the tranquillity. Within

Sculpture, Rydal

this garden are two large pieces of stone, which are being worked on by Josefina and her students from time to time.

¤ As the bridge over the beck is reached, there is a fine view of the lower Rydal waterfall, much described in 18th and 19th century literature and painted by, among others, John Constable, Joseph Wright of Derby and Julius Ceasar Ibbetson. Between bridge and waterfall is an unassuming stone-built hut, known as the Grotto. This hut is of historic importance, as a very early example (1669) of a "viewing house". The window in the rear wall faces the falls, framing a well-composed "picture". The Grotto has been renovated in recent years; it is used as a chapel and is, unfortunately, not open to the public.

¤ After the bridge, turn left, uphill, and divert up a ramp marked "to the barn and barn parking". Away to the right are large camping areas; visible is a chestnut tree which is said to require twenty-four cub scouts with linked hands to encircle the girth of the trunk. Return down the ramp and bear right, following the signed footpath among the outbuildings of the Hall. Former workshops and a sawmill are now a youth centre and a camp shop, but the most interesting of all is the stone barn, recently converted into a spacious conference and meeting hall, named after Bishop Bulley, whose initiative secured the buildings and grounds for the Diocese. The building nearest the beck houses a turbine which provides electricity for the whole complex.

¤ Re-cross the beck above the falls, pausing on the bridge to see the 18th century game larder, a curious wishing well-like structure used to hang game. The top section would have been meshed to keep out birds and other creatures. Continue along the public footpath round the back of the Hall, passing both the oldest part of the structure and the tea room, which is open to the public daily from Easter until the autumn half term holiday (weekends in winter until Christmas). Rejoin the road, turning left to return to the start.

7. Grasmere

Description

As one of the best-loved and most accessible Lakeland villages, in high season Grasmere inevitably suffers from its own popularity. It is, nevertheless, still a most attractive place, beautifully situated at the head of its lake and ringed by wonderful mountain scenery, even though Thomas Grey's "a little unsuspected paradise" (1769) is now hardly true. There is much for visitors, particularly those with an interest in William Wordsworth and other literary figures of the time.

The Trail

The green at the centre of the village provides an unmistakeable starting place. On one corner is Sam Read's bookshop, familiar to generations of those who like to browse among and to buy their Wainwrights and other Lakeland books as near as possible to the heart of the district. Across the road the Heaton Cooper gallery displays the work of three generations of this talented family, with an eye-catching array of mainly, but not entirely, local scenes. On the far side, the Red Lion Inn was described as "an old fashioned little place" in 1854.

¤   Walk past the public conveniences along the little one-way street to the road junction by the Wordsworth Hotel (named compara-

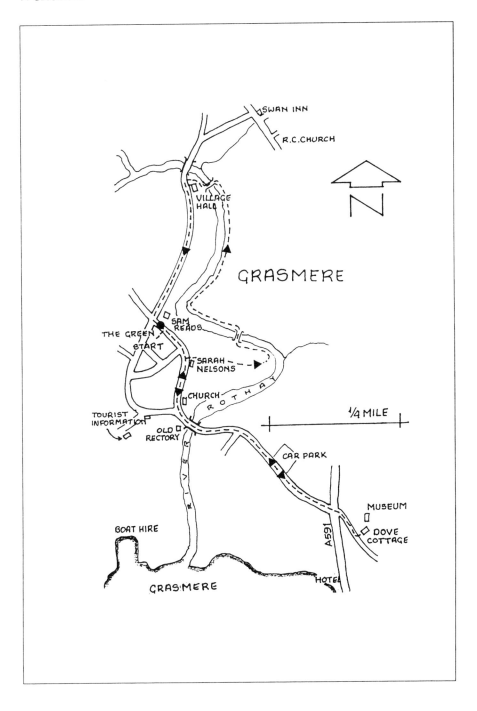

The boat landings, Grasmere

tively recently and nothing to do with the poet). Straight ahead
is St Oswald's Church, but first comes the tiny bakehouse and
shop, formerly the village schoolhouse, which is the only source
of the celebrated Grasmere gingerbread. Started over 100 years
ago by Sarah Nelson, production of this delicacy has continued
ever since. The recipe is a closely guarded secret. Across the road
are another picture gallery displaying and selling the work of a
locally based artist, and the National Trust shop, in premises
which were formerly an inn.

¤   At first impression, St Oswald's Church, commenced in the 13th
century and much modified since, is disappointing, largely because of the drab, unappealing, cement rendering. Inside, however, the church is much better, with its curiously attractive
lopsidedness resulting from the addition of a north aisle. There
are other items to seek out indoors but, for the great majority of
the visitors, the real magnet here is the close association with
nature's own poet, the incomparable William Wordsworth.
Within hearing of the gently lapping waters of the adjacent River

Rothay, in the far corner of the churchyard are the graves of several of the Wordsworth family, including William himself, marked by simple stones. The less fortunate Hartley Coleridge lies close by.

¤ Across the road from the church is the Rectory, Wordsworth's home from 1811 to 1813, not the most happy period of his life. Two of his children died here at the ages of 3 years and 6 years respectively and lie buried opposite. Small wonder that he left the village in 1813, moving to Rydal Mount for the last 37 years of his life.

¤ Adjacent is the Grasmere garden centre, which has the Tourist Information Office tucked away behind. [The minor road to Redbank and Elterwater also leads in approximately a quarter of a mile to the only place on the lake where rowing boats may be hired by the hour].

¤ Continue along the village street, cross the river, and head for the main road, passing the clothing sale premises where Chris Reekie formerly plied his loom watched by the customers. The fine mountains ahead and to the left are part of the Fairfield group; from the left; Stone Arthur, with Great Rigg behind; Heron Pike; and Nab Scar, above Rydal. On the left, behind the car and coach park, is the sports field, home of the world famous Grasmere Sports, Lakeland's best-known traditional gathering held every August since 1861. Cumberland wrestling, fell running ("guides' race"), and hound trailing are all included.

¤ Cross the main road to the outlying hamlet of Town End. A little way up the minor road is Dove Cottage, Mecca for all pilgrims of Wordsworth and the galaxy of literary talent which gathered here around this extraordinarily gifted man. His nine years in residence, from 1799 to 1808, at this simple little house saw the genius of the young poet come to full fruition as he wandered, free-spirited, over the fells and by the lakes which he loved so well, or meditated in the garden which his devoted sister Dorothy tended so lovingly. Southey, Coleridge, de Quincey, and Walter Scott were among the distinguished visitors.

¤   The cottage is still much as it was when Wordsworth left; addi-
    tionally, an adjacent barn has been converted into a museum.
    Both are open to the public, except from mid-January to mid-Feb-
    ruary. There is a tea room nearby. The road by the cottage was
    the main road from Ambleside to Grasmere before the present
    highway along the side of the lake was constructed during
    Wordsworth's lifetime, and much to his annoyance.

¤   Re-cross the main road to return towards the village. The rather
    shapeless mountain to the left is the bulky Silver Howe; almost
    straight ahead is Grasmere's own mountain, the sharp little peak
    of Helm Crag. Just visible below, to the left of Helm Crag, is Allan
    Bank, a sizeable house of 1805, painted in a light colour and so
    conspicuous in the landscape that Wordsworth was extremely
    critical; his dislike was, however, not sufficient to prevent him
    moving into the house in 1808 when his expanding family out-
    grew Dove Cottage. Before moving on to the Rectory in 1811, he
    softened the landscape impact of Allan Bank by planting trees
    below the house, many of which are still there.

¤   Pass the church and, before reaching the Wordsworth Hotel, turn
    right into a well-made footpath along the side of the river. Cross-
    ing the river twice, this path provides an enjoyable stroll to the
    northern end of the village, rejoining the road by the village hall,
    used for many exhibitions of craft and art works. Turn left to
    return along the road to the village green.

Footpath, Grasmere

8. Hawkshead

Description

Until comparatively recent times Hawkshead was a largely self-sufficient small town, well off the beaten track and comparatively difficult of access. Originally established as a centre for the local wool and timber-related trades by the monks of Furness Abbey, following the dissolution of that Abbey by Henry VIII in 1537, the town was granted a market and became important in its own right, trading widely by means of pack horses.

Since World War II the scene has changed dramatically, as visitors in large numbers now readily find their way to this formerly remote town. A road by-pass has greatly improved conditions in the centre, but the southern end, with the car park which is large but still inadequate at busy times, and the proliferation of sizeable shops established solely to attract tourists, is quite out of sympathy with the original town (or should it now be 'village'?).

Despite these problems, Hawkshead remains quite unlike any other Lakeland town or village. White painted buildings, many of considerable antiquity, cluster tightly around linked squares and narrow cobbled road and alleyways. It is a wonderful place to wander, with enticing photographic opportunities at every corner, whilst the Wordsworth and Beatrix Potter associations provide added interest for so many visitors, not least those from overseas. It has been suggested that there is a certain sense of artificial preservation, an "owned by the National Trust" feeling about Hawkshead. One has only to observe the development of the south end of the village or to think of the worst parts of Bowness in order to realise that the presumed alternative of allowing free rein to commercial interests would be disastrous.

The setting of the village among some of Lakeland's more gentle hill country and close to the shore of tranquil Esthwaite Water is entirely pleasant, with long views to the Helvellyn and Fairfield mountain groups to the north.

Hawkshead village

The Trail

The most likely parking place is the pay and display car park accessed from the by-pass road. Start from here by walking past the information centre and the public conveniences, crossing the village street to the former Grammar School.

¤ This historic school was founded in 1585 by locally-born Edward Sandys, who had progressed to become Archbishop of York. The present building dates from 1675, as attested by a plaque over the entrance. Rather surprisingly, it continued in use until 1909. There is public access (on payment) to the interior, but only from Easter to October. The star exhibit is William Wordsworth's desk, authenticated for posterity by his juvenile vandalism. Young Wordsworth was a pupil here from 1779 to 1787. Upstairs is the school library, including Archbishop Sandys's personal copy of the "Bishop's Bible", which he had helped to translate. Wordsworth's brother John's name is carved on one of the window sills.

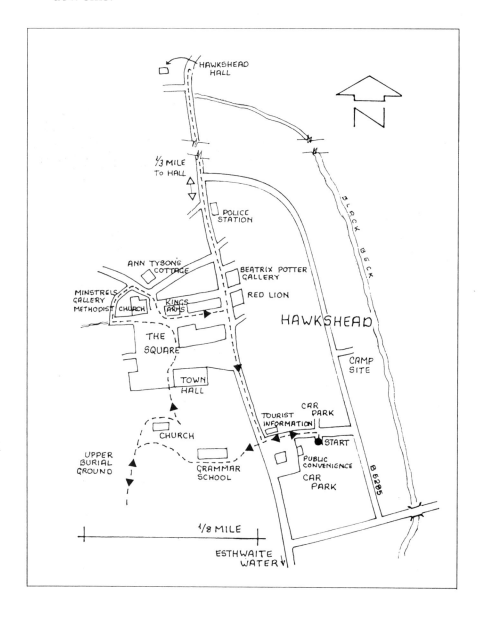

¤ From the Grammar School continue uphill towards the church of St Michael and All Angels, beautifully situated on a knoll above, but still in close contact with the members of its flock in the village below. The elevated churchyard is a fine place for views over the rooftops; carry on up the steps to the left to reach the far end of the higher burial ground for the best views of the mountains and a glimpse of Esthwaite Water. Several of the slate on edge field boundary divisions, so characteristic of the Hawkshead area, can also be seen.

¤ There has been a church on this site since early medieval times; the small nave was extended around 1300 and the present side aisles were added around 1500. The tower is more than 700 years old. The white painted rough-cast which covered the external walls – Wordsworth's "snow white church upon her hill" – and which must have harmonised well with the village buildings, was removed in 1875/6. As might be expected, the church features more than once in the great man's poems, as does Hawkshead generally and the surrounding district. It is not difficult to appreciate that at this formative stage of his life, as he rambled extensively in this beautiful countryside, young William's ultra sensitive personality was soaking up every facet of nature, ranging from the most minute particular, the sunlit raindrop on the blade of grass, to the mighty, the mountain peak set against the stormy sky, all providing a deep well of experience on which he could and would draw for inspiration. His vision of humanity was as an indivisible part of this wonderful and manifest nature.

¤ Inside, the church is light and well-proportioned, with the slight irregularity of pillars and arches adding to its attraction. Many and varied memorial plaques might possibly provide some diversion to the congregation should the sermon be dull. The Sandys family private chapel has effigies of the parents of the Archbishop and of a later member, Col. Thomas Myles Sandys. On the opposite side of the chancel is a primitive dug out chest constructed nearly 400 years ago when each parish had to provide secure housing for the parish register. The chest is probably part of a tie beam removed when the roof was raised to accommodate the present clerestory, an early and ingenious example of Do-It-

Street scene, Hawkshead

Yourself, as the internal space may well be an enlargement of the hole originally cut to take the foot of a king post.

¤   Before descending to the village, walk to the east end of the church, where a stone bench along the outside wall has for centuries been a place for villagers to sit and to pass the time of day. The Square is entered by the side of the Town Hall, built in 1790 and enlarged in honour of Queen Victoria's Jubilee in 1887. The building included Assembly Rooms and a ground floor arcade, now filled in, which was occupied as a "shambles" by local butchers on market days.

¤   Ahead is the Kings Arms, one of several historic hostelries in Hawkshead, with the equally ancient Minstrel's Gallery teashop and the unusual Methodist Church to the left. Pass to the left of the Methodist Church, along an alleyway. The stream visible here is covered by flag stones as is passes under the street surface, hence the name Flag Street. Turn right by Flag Cottage, along a very narrow passage, to reach a lane; turn right to Ann Tyson's Cottage. Despite a fair amount of dispute, it does seem that

William Wordsworth and other boys from the Grammar School lodged here with Ann Tyson from 1779-83, before she moved to the hamlet of Colthouse a short distance along the road to Sawrey. The claim that Wordsworth worshipped at an adjacent chapel is more dubious.

¤   Bear right, under the arch, to reach Main Street, by the Red Lion Inn. Look for the two carved figures high on the building, one depicting a farmer taking his pig to market and the other of a man holding the whistle which was blown at market opening time. The inn is claimed to be a 15th century coaching house, making it one of the oldest buildings in the village.

¤   Beside the inn is the Beatrix Potter Gallery, owned by the National Trust, housed in the former office of Beatrix Potter's husband, William Heelis, a local solicitor. The gallery, open from Easter to October each year, has a collection exceeding 500 of Beatrix Potter's original watercolours and drawings which provided such attractive illustrations for the famous books. The display, varied each year, includes approximately 80 of these works. Enthusiasts might be able to recognise some of the buildings of Hawkshead which provide the background to the figures in the illustrations of several of the books. Next door to the gallery is the quaintly-named Bend or Bump Cottage.

¤   Further along Main Street to the north is the large, solidly Victorian court house and police station.

¤   [For an extension of the trail, pass the police station and continue along the road for rather more than ¼ mile to a road junction. On the far side is the site of Hawkshead Hall, erected by the Furness Abbey monks as the administrative centre for their activities in this area. Only the former gate-house, known as the Old Court house from a subsequent use, survives, in the care of the National Trust. There is little to see inside this ancient building, but access is allowed without charge, the key being available at the National Trust shop in the village.]

¤   From the Beatrix Potter Gallery, head back along Main Street towards the car park.

9. Cartmel

Description

The term "Cumbria's Cathedral City in miniature" has been used to describe what, in size, is little more than a village, clustered close to, and dominated by, the great Priory Church. Cartmel Priory was founded by William Marshall, Earl of Pembroke, in 1188/9 for Augustinian canons and was constructed during the following years with, inevitably, later additions and alterations.

At the dissolution of the monasteries from 1537, the structure of the church largely survived because the parishioners persuaded Henry's commissioners that it was needed to serve as the church for the parish. Surprisingly, the gate-house to the Priory also survived and is now the dominant feature of the village square.

The River Eea, scarcely more than a stream, flows through the middle of Cartmel, a reminder that many centuries ago much of this low lying land was under water. Almost as historic as the Priory are the Cartmel Races, according to local legend originating as Whitsun recreation for the monks. The Bank Holiday meetings on this smallest of race-courses are popular festive occasions bringing crowds from far and wide. The annual agricultural show is similarly esteemed.

Apart from race meeting and show days, until very recent times Cartmel was regarded as a quiet backwater, to be sought out by the discerning, perhaps at times when the Lake District proper would be overrun with visitors. While in comparative terms this is still true, very many people do now find their way to this charming little place and summer weekends are anything but quiet. So far, however, it has been spared the worst manifestations of commercial development.

Cartmel Priory

The Trail

From whatever direction Cartmel is approached, drive through the village square to the large car parking area on the race course. Walk back along the narrow access road to the Square. Here, there are fish dressing slabs and the remains of the market cross, overlooked by the bulk of the Priory gate-house, two old inns, and varied shops including a well-known second hand bookshop. All in all, a most attractive combination. The gate-house is in the care of the National Trust; at first floor level is a gallery used for exhibitions.

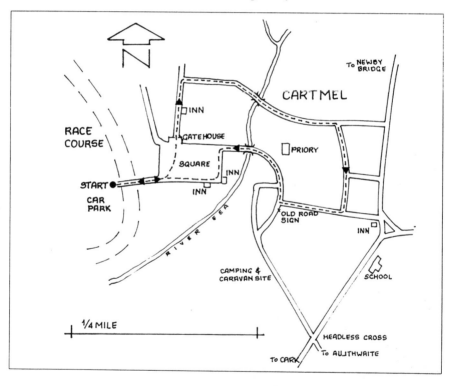

¤ Proceed under the gate-house, passing the Cavendish Arms, claimed to be Cartmel's oldest inn, with a dated horse mounting block, and Cartmel Brewery. On the corner where the road (and Trail) bend to the right there is an enamel "Raleigh the all steel bicycle" sign, a rare survival.

¤ The river is crossed at Wheelhouse Bridge of 1815 and the lane continues across the back of the Priory. In front is the limestone bulk of Hampsfell, separating Cartmel from the nearby Grange over Sands, on Morecambe Bay. Take the first roadway on the right, at the end of the Priory grounds, to pass attractive cottages and gardens, with a Victorian post box on the left. Turn right at the next junction, then right again by St Mary's Lodge and Tea Room. At this latter junction is an old milestone giving distances to Lancaster and Ulverston "over sands" i.e. across Morecambe Bay.

¤ The climax of this Trail is, inevitably, the Priory. On approach, the eye is first taken by the belfry of 1410, set diagonally on top of the squat central tower. Next, on the left, is a door with holes claimed to have been made by bullets fired either at or by Cromwell's soldiers when they camped in the building for a night in 1643. The organ and some furnishings were vandalised at the same time.

¤ The light and lofty interior of the church is reached by a Norman doorway. To the left is a sculpture of the Holy Family by Josefina de Vasconcellos (see the Rydal Trail, page 35), followed by the impressive Cavendish memorial, and then a brass plaque in memory of Roland Briggs, who founded a still surviving charity

for the distribution of bread every Sunday to indigent housekeep-
ers in the parish.

¤   The richly decorated oak chancel screen is claimed to be one of
the finest examples of 17th century woodwork in England.
Equally fine are the miseres, nearly 200 years older, which adorn
the seats in the choir stalls, a treasure house of the imagination
of the medieval woodcarvers. Excessive weathering of the bench
ends is a reminder that at the dissolution at least part of the roof
was removed and was not replaced for 80 years. The great east
window was also damaged, but does retain some coloured glass.
Some of the missing glass is believed to have found its way to St
Martin's Church in Bowness (see the Bowness Trail, page 15).

¤   Beside the chancel, in the south aisle, a Josefina bronze of St
Michael stands close to the ornate 14th century tomb of Sir John
Harrington and his wife Joan.

¤   The River Eea is crossed again, by Church Bridge, on the return
to the Square and car park.

10. Ulverston

Description

By Cumbrian standards Ulverston is a good-sized market town, situated to the south of the Lake District, about half way along the main coastal road to Barrow. Although not particularly pretty, and in part somewhat run down, this former Lancashire town does have an agreeable old fashioned character, with its cobbled square and good selection of small, individual, shops, best seen amid the bustle on one of the market days. The market charter was granted by Edward I in 1280 and the market is now held each Thursday and Saturday.

Ulverston has a history of industrial prosperity stretching back to monastic times, when Furness Abbey was all-powerful in the district. Following the construction of a short canal by John Rennie in 1795, the town became a small but busy port, with a minor shipbuilding industry. For some years early in the 19th century more than 500 ships per annum visited the port. This was a particularly prosperous time, but there has since been an inevitable decline as Barrow has gained in importance and, after the arrival of the Furness Railway in 1844, the canal was allowed to become silted. There are now several modern industries and a long established local brewery.

Although outside Lakeland proper, the town is well-placed between the mountains and the sands of Morecambe Bay; road communications have been improved in recent years and the rail services linking to the west coast main line at Lancaster and beyond have been enhanced.

Of particular interest are the Cumbria Crystal glass factory, open to visitors, and with a well-stocked shop, and the unique little museum which commemorates one of the town's most famous sons – Stanley Laurel, born here in 1890, who went on to become half of the most celebrated comedy duo of all time. Interesting buildings include the handsome, surprisingly Italianate Trustee Savings Bank in Market Street, and a former corn mill in Mill Street.

The Trustee Savings Bank , Ulverston

Dominating the town on the steep-sided Hoad Hill is a two-third size replica of the Eddystone lighthouse, erected in 1850 as a monument to Sir John Barrow, the noted explorer, born in Ulverston in 1764.

The Trail

Approaching by car from the east, turn right into Brewery Street at a large roundabout. There is a pay and display car park on the left, at Union Place.

¤ Start here. Across Brewery Street is Hartley's, the long established local brewery. Walk along Brewery Street, turn right at Hart Street, then left at Ford Park Crescent. Follow this road to the top and then turn right at a lane in front of St Mary's Hospice, soon reaching a gate which gives access to open land.

¤ The monument is now high above. Note the very restricted hours of opening for refreshments displayed by the gate, and the curious arrangement whereby a red flag is flown when open. The path climbs steeply, but is surfaced for most of the way and is well-provided with seats. The are obvious route variations, but to go a little way beyond the tower and then to loop back seems to offer the easiest gradients.

¤ The lighthouse replica is quite impressive, but best of all are the views – from the contentious windmills on Kirkby Moor to the north, round over the Leven Estuary with Chapel Island, and across the vast sandy expanse of Morecambe Bay then, at shorter range, the roof tops of Ulverston, including the top basin of the former canal. All in all, well worth the effort if time and energy are sufficient.

¤ For a direct descent, go straight along the top of the hill, roughish in places. A fairly worn path keeps close to the wall on the right, descending steeply to the gate.

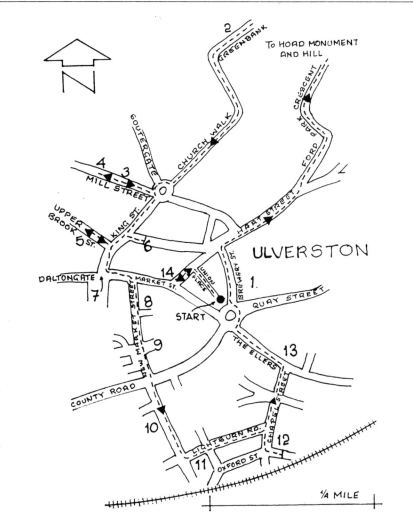

Key:

1. Hartley's Brewery
2. St Mary's Church
3. Ulverston Point Craft Centre
4. Heron Glass
5. Laurel & Hardy Museum
6. Heritage Centre
7. War Memorial/Market Cross
8. Market Hall
9. Coronation Hall/Tourist Information
10. Classic Motor
11. Cumbria Crystal
12. Stan Laurel's birthplace
13. Stan Laurel Inn
14. Trustee Savings Bank

¤   [To add a short country walk, take the farm track bearing right,
     later looping back left to reach the edge of the town a little way
     north of St Mary's Church.]

¤   From the gate return along the lane. directly to St Mary's Church-
     yard. The parish church has a little Norman work evident. but is
     largely a Victorian reconstruction. although the 16th century
     tower has escaped renovation. From the churchyard carry on
     down Church Walk to a mini roundabout. Bear right into Mill
     Street, following a "Glass blowing factory" signpost. The Ulver-
     ston Point Craft Centre, with tea and coffee bar and garden, is on
     the right in 50 yards, occupying a converted granary. Heron Glass,
     with factory shop, is a few yards further.

¤   Return to the mini roundabout and turn right to continue along
     King Street. Turn right into Upper Brook Street; the Laurel and
     Hardy Museum is on the right in a few yards. Back to King Street
     and cross over into an alleyway, one of the old yards of the town.
     On the right is a small, privately-owned heritage centre; a small
     charge is made for entry

¤   Return to King Street, turning left to the top of the Market Place
     and the Market Cross, actually a War Memorial designed by W.G.
     Collingwood, which replaced an earlier cross. Walk down the
     Market Place and turn right into New Market Street. At the
     entrance to the Market Hall is a plaque giving a potted history of
     the building. Follow the street as far as a roundabout; on the left
     is the post office and then the Coronation Hall. which houses the
     Tourist Information Centre.

¤   With suitable care, cross the A590. After passing the library, the
     Classic Motorcycle Museum is on the right (open 10am to 4.30pm,
     closed Sundays and Mondays). Continue in the same direction.
     Turn left at Lightburn Road to reach Cumbria Crystal (factory
     open Monday to Thursday 9am to 4pm, Friday 9am to 3pm The
     shop opens for slightly longer hours, also on Sunday and Bank
     Holiday afternoons). Both factory and shop entrances are round
     the back.

¤ Proceed to the far end of Lighburn Road. At Chapel Street turn right, then left into Argyle Street. On the sixteenth of June 1890, Stanley Laurel was born at no. 3, a modest terraced house. Return along Chapel Street to the Ellers. Across the road is the Stan Laurel Inn. Follow the Ellers to the main A590 road, at a large roundabout. The car park is right opposite.

The Laurel and Hardy Museum

¤   However, before leaving, it would be a pity to miss out the Trustee Savings Bank building, which is close by. Go through Union Place and turn left for a few yards along Union Street. The fine structure, erected in 1838, had its clock, with a bell weighing no less than 14 cwt, added in 1845.

11. Coniston

Description

The large village of Coniston is beautifully situated close to the lake of the same name, and at the foot of that much loved mountain, Coniston Old Man. Early days as a farming settlement, with Coniston Old Hall dominant, were followed by the opening of copper mines, probably late in the 15th century, mainly in the area now known as Copper Mines Valley. This industry was considerably developed in the 19th century. Also in the 19th century slate quarrying became important locally and the Furness Railway branch line from Foxfield to Coniston was opened in 1859, primarily to provide transport for these industries. Boats on the lake had previously been used to carry bulk materials.

Today the economy of the village is mainly dependent on tourism although its industrial origins are still very apparent and the village centre is hardly pretty.

Coniston Old Hall is a remarkable survival. Claimed by some to be based on a 13th century pele tower and by others to be of 16th century origin, it is quite unlike any other building although many of the elements such as the chimneys and the cart ramp to the first floor granary are entirely typical of Lakeland vernacular architecture. Admired by both Wordsworth and Coleridge, it also formed part of the view enjoyed by Ruskin from his house at Brantwood, across the lake. The Hall was the home of the Le Fleming family (see the Rydal trail, page 33) for very many years.

Brantwood is a spectacularly situated 18th century house which has had numerous additions in the ensuing years. In 1871 it was purchased, unseen, by John Ruskin, the great philosopher, poet, painter, and social reformer of the late 19th century, remaining his home until his death in 1900. Well worth visiting for the collection of Ruskin's drawings and paintings, the house interior retains a 19th century ambience. It is open to the public daily from mid-March to mid-November and on a more restricted basis during the winter. A shop and refreshments are provided.

Coniston Old Hall

The Trail

A good place to park and to start the trail is the small car park high above the village on the site of the former railway station (the line closed in 1962), reached by Station Road, climbing steeply from the village street.

¤   Return downhill towards the village centre, and turn left at a road junction, opposite the site of an 1882 drinking trough "come all ye that thirst", now converted into a seat. The Sun Inn was one of Coniston's several old inns, greatly enlarged in 1902. Continue to the main street and turn left over the bridge, keeping left into Yewdale Road. The Black Bull is an attractive 16th century hostelry, patronised by Coleridge and De Quincey.

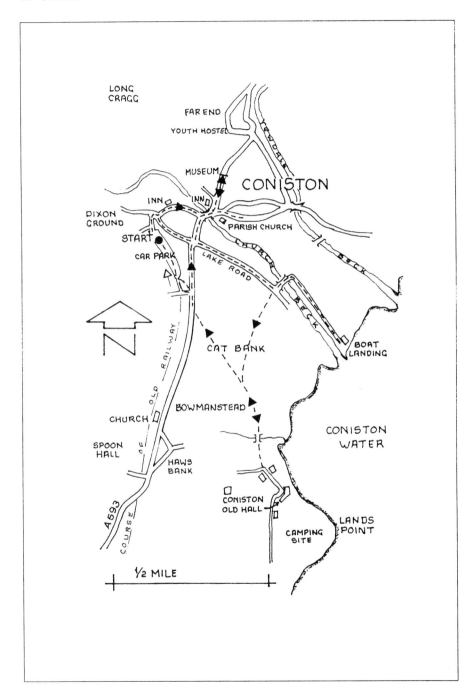

The Black Bull

¤ A short distance further, on the left, is the village institute with
   the Ruskin museum at the rear, open daily during the holiday
   season, except on Saturdays. Here, a fascinating collection of
   Ruskin's personal belongings has been assembled, together with
   exhibits illustrating his local projects, such as "Ruskin lace".
   There are plans to enlarge this museum in the fairly near future.

¤ Return as far as the left turn into Tilberthwaite Avenue. The
   parish church of St Andrew is on the site of an older chapel. The
   nave and tower of the present building date from 1819, whilst the
   chancel and vestry were added in 1891, when the opportunity
   was also taken to carry out a general renovation. The grave and
   memorial of John Ruskin (1819-1900) is situated at the back of
   the churchyard. The column, in Tilberthwaite stone, was carved
   by a local craftsman to designs by W.G. Collingwood, the eminent
   local historian who was, for many years, Ruskin's secretary. The
   scenes on the column depict Ruskin's interests – the Guild of St
   George craft organisation, poetry, music, nature, science, and
   some of his principal writings, such as the Seven Lamps of
   Architecture and the Stones of Venice.

¤ From the church continue along Tilberthwaite Avenue to its junction with Ruskin Avenue. Here stands a very different memorial, that to the Campbell family who brought a great deal of publicity to the area in the 1950s and '60s, with both Malcolm and, later, his son Donald making attempts on the world water speed record on Coniston Water in the Bluebird speedboats. Successful in 1955, the saga ended tragically with Donald's death in 1967.

¤ Return to the main street, turn left and then left again into Lake Road to head for Coniston Water. The road kinks to cross Church Beck by the modern Lake Road Workshops complex.

¤ [To cruise on *Gondola*, hire a boat, or take the ferry crossing to Brantwood, continue along the road to the lake shore. *Gondola* is a Victorian steam launch beautifully restored and operated by the National Trust. The ferry calls at several landing points in both directions along the lake; out of season the service is very restricted.]

¤ The Trail goes over the stile by the gate on the village side of the workshops complex, turning right to follow an obvious footpath along the edge of the field. The destination is Coniston Old Hall which has, at present, an apparently not altogether happy mixed use as a farmhouse and the office/reception for a camping/caravan site. After admiring the historic building, return along the main drive, forking left in approximately ½ mile on to a footpath close to a plantation, reaching a gate followed by a ladder stile, and slanting upwards towards the main road. Join the road at a stile and turn right.

¤ To return to the car park there is a choice; either to follow the main road and turn left into Station Road, or to turn left in 100 yards or so, then bearing right along the hillside, passing the terraced cottages dating from Coniston's industrial past, before reaching the site of the former station.

12. Ravenglass

Description

A lthough remotely situated, to the west of the Lake District proper, Ravenglass was an important port in Roman times. Glanovanta fort occupied a site a little way to the south of the present village, and the surviving structure of the bath house, known as Walls Castle, is claimed to be the highest above ground genuinely Roman building in England. Glanovanta was linked by road to the fort at Galava (Ambleside), via Hardknott.

The access to the port has long been silted, and the village has just one street, leading most attractively directly to the shore of the estuary, where the Rivers Esk, Mite, and Irt combine.

A mile or so from the village, close to the bulk of Muncaster Fell, is Muncaster Castle. Originally a 14th century defensive pele tower, much enlarged by the addition of a mansion in the 19th century, this beautifully sited estate has been the home of the Pennington family since 1208. There are strong associations with King Henry VI who was sheltered here by Sir John Pennington in 1464 after his defeat at the battle of Hexham. In gratitude the King gave Sir John a small green glass bowl, decorated with gold, known as the "luck" of Muncaster. The legend is that as long as the "luck" remains intact, so the Pennington family will prosper. A replica is on display at the castle.

The castle gardens, being rich in rhododendrons, are particularly good in spring and early summer, and the views are splendid. Within the grounds is an owl sanctuary with one of the world's finest collections, and the church of St Michael, with battlemented walls and a nave believed to have survived from the 12th century. In the churchyard are fragments of Saxon crosses, while inside are memorials to the Pennington family. The gardens and owl centre are open daily throughout the year. The castle is open Tuesday to Sunday (and Bank Holidays) during the afternoon from late March to late October.

Muncaster Mill

The Whitehaven and Furness Junction Railway (later part of the Furness Railway) was opened to Ravenglass in July 1849. There are still passenger services north to Whitehaven and Carlisle and south to Barrow. Beside the station is the terminus and headquarters of the much-loved La'al Ratty, the Ravenglass and Eskdale Railway, the narrow gauge line which runs for more than seven miles through lovely countryside to Dalegarth in Eskdale. Originally of 3' gauge, and constructed primarily for iron ore traffic, the railway deteriorated steadily and was closed in 1908. Re-laid to the present 15" gauge, it re-opened a few years later and is now a major visitor attraction.

The first station from Ravenglass is at Muncaster Mill, a restored water powered corn mill which is in regular use. Freshly milled products are on sale at the mill, which is open to visitors daily from April to October.

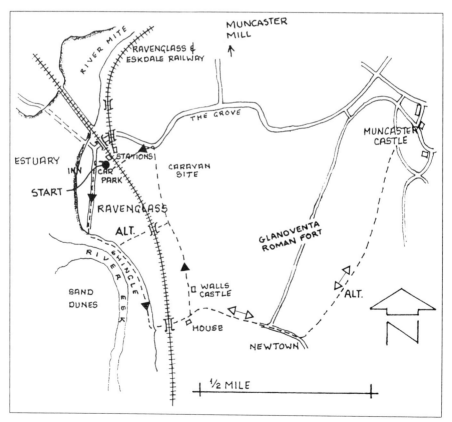

The Trail

Start at the public car park, signposted from the village street. Walk back to the street and turn left, passing a small hotel, tea shop, and many former fishermen's cottages before reaching the ramp at the end. Notice the business-like steel flood gates which protect the buildings against flooding by particularly high tides.

¤ From the ramp follow a signposted bridleway across the back of the beach. [If the tide is high, this might be impassable in whole or in part, in which case alternatives will be suggested]. The path is somewhat rough underfoot but there is no real difficulty. Follow the blue arrow on a post a little way along the foreshore then, in about half a mile, turn left at a post with a yellow arrow to pass under the railway line.

¤ Turn left again along a wooded lane. Pass a large house dated 1885, and bear left at a junction to reach Walls Castle. This former bath house is just a small ruin, but there is a helpful interpretation board.

¤ Continue along the lane and, immediately before reaching the main road, turn left at a "public footpath to railway station and Ravenglass" signpost. This little path leads directly to the beautifully trim terminus of the Ravenglass and Eskdale Railway. Turn right before the footbridge to descend to the platforms. The station is equipped with tea bar, toilets, information centre/shop and there is a short video which gives an introduction to the railway.

¤ Return over the footbridge to the car park. The Ratty Arms inn occupies the former station building on the main railway line.

¤ [Should the tide have covered most of the bridleway, it might still be possible to cross the first short stretch of beach and then turn left by the first post with arrows, to go under the railway. On reaching the lane, turn right to walk to Walls Castle. Should even this limited use of the bridleway not be possible, the footbridge over the railway line can be used to start the trail, turning right at the far end to slant across to join the lane close to the railway bridge mentioned above]

Ravenglass Station

¤ [To visit Muncaster Castle, the choice is between extending the trail by an extra mile in each direction (unless, of course, there is a non-walking driver in the party), and driving along the main road. To extend the trail, turn sharp right after passing the big house (before reaching Walls Castle). Continue as far as Newtown farmstead, turning left at a permissive path which passes through a coniferous plantation. Above the plantation the path is not well-defined as it rises across the rough pasture. Keep a little to the left of a knoll, aiming for a gate in the Muncaster Castle boundary wall. From the gate there is a good footpath downhill to the castle itself.

¤ Return by the same route to rejoin the basic trail just short of Walls Castle]

¤ To visit Muncaster Mill, there is no recommendable footpath. From Ravenglass drive for a total of ½ mile, firstly on the village road, then the A595 to the north, turning right into the mill's own trackway just before the main road crosses the River Mite. There is car parking space close to the mill.

¤ Preferably, use the La'al Ratty!

13. Whitehaven

Description

To those who are unfamiliar with the West Cumberland coast, the sizable town of Whitehaven can come as something of a surprise. Prior to the mid-17th century Whitehaven was nothing more than a tiny fishing village. Subsequent development of the port and the creation of a shipbuilding industry, both by the Lowther family, were so successful that within a few years it was claimed to be the third busiest port, ranking below only London and Bristol.

The port development was linked to the exploitation of rich local deposits of coal and iron ore, increasing steadily during the 18th and 19th centuries. Some coal mines extended for several miles beneath the sea bed and were among the largest in the country. Other industries, such as the chemical plant on the nearby hill, followed. As the port prospered, the town was laid out on a grid pattern with terraces of elegant 18th century houses, many of which remain today. The castle at one end of Lowther Street was built as the home of the Lowther family in the mid-17th century, later becoming a hospital, now superseded by a more modern building on the edge of town. The grounds, known as Castle Park, are used for public recreation.

One little niche in history remains secure: Whitehaven was the last place in Britain to be attacked by American naval forces. On 23rd. April 1778, during the American War of Independence, the privateer John Paul Jones, with a roving commission to harass ports in Britain, arrived in Whitehaven with the intention of setting the whole merchant fleet on fire. After rowing ashore he spiked some of the guns of the harbour defence battery and attempted, without much success, to fire the ships. The alarm was raised and he retreated forthwith.

Sadly, the port has declined to a shadow of its former importance and has a neglected, rather desolate, air. Shipbuilding ceased before the end of the 19th century, and the last coal mine closed in 1985. The town does, however, retain a fair amount of its character and efforts are being made to tidy up some of the inevitable dereliction. The shopping centre is partially pedestrianised and the market place comes vigorously to life with Thursday and Saturday markets.

The Trail

There are free car parking spaces along the side of the South Harbour, accessed from Strand Street, which is part of the one way traffic system. Start here.

¤ Walk away from the town along the harbourside, which is part of the Cumbria Coastal Way. On the left are varied relics of the Wellington coal mine, most notably the "candlestick" ventilation shaft, an elaborate chimney-like structure on the hillside above. A cannon spiked by John Paul Jones still faces out to sea, as the path loops back to the left, rising towards the "candlestick" above.

The "Candlestick" and outer harbour

¤ At the top of the path a diversion for 30 yards to the right reveals a plaque to the memory of the men, women, and children who lost their lives in the Whitehaven and district collieries. Back on course, the route now heads towards the town, passing the coastguard building, which is the refurbished former lodge to the Wellington pit, operational from 1840 to 1933.

¤   Cross over the narrow track bed of a long disused inclined plane
    which must have fed coal directly to the harbour, and continue
    towards the town, enjoying the splendid views. A rather neglected
    structure on the left was the fan house to the mine which provided
    the vast quantities of fresh air needed below ground. It has been
    preserved as a memorial to the 100 or so miners killed in a
    particularly disastrous underground explosion.

¤   Angle down Rosemary Lane past a 19th century Mission Hall to
    reach the busy Strand Street. Cross over, turn right and then left
    into Irish Street, which has some good Georgian houses. Turn left
    at Cross Street, where a plaque on the wall immediately after the
    junction records that the house (no. 5) was built by Mathias Reed,
    the "father of painting in Cumberland". Turn right, and then right
    again at Roper Street. In a few yards, on the right is Michael
    Moon's bookshop, a sprawling treasure house for browsers. Mi-
    chael Moon not only sells books old and new, but also publishes
    new editions of local books long out of print.

¤   Return to the junction of Roper Street and Queen Street and turn
    right, facing St James's Church at long distance. Lowther Street is
    soon reached. Opposite is the Tower of the former St Nicholas
    Church, now used as a community centre/cafe, and the survivor
    of a fire which destroyed the remainder of the church in 1971.
    The spacious churchyard and gardens are attractively laid out,
    forming a valuable open space in the middle of town. George
    Washington's grandmother is buried here.

¤   Continue along Queen Street (or through the gardens alongside),
    heading directly for St James's Church with its lofty position on
    the edge of town. You must go inside to appreciate this lovely
    18th century church, basically Georgian in style. There is a
    beautiful altar piece by a pupil of Correggio, decorated ceiling,
    and interesting windows.

¤   Turn right on leaving the church, fork left to descend Wellington
    Row, and go right at the bottom to reach Tangier Street. Carry on
    to Duke Street, turning left then right into the pedestrianised King
    Street, heart of the shopping centre and leading directly to the
    Market Place. The former Market Hall, neglected for many years,

now houses a Tourist Information Office. From the Market Place turn right to cross Strand Street and reach the harbour, continuing along the quay towards the car parking area. The building with a white, circular, portion is the Beacon Heritage Centre, which has taken over the function of the former local museum.

The Old Market Hall

14. Maryport

Description

Although Maryport has inevitably shared in the general industrial and economic decline of the West Cumberland coastal area, the once busy little port and town, with its neat grid iron street pattern, is well worth the attention of the visitor. Successful efforts are being made in re-developing parts of the run-down harbour area, with recreation and tourism prominent.

Maryport

The Trail

Start at the point where modern Maryport itself started in 1749, the Maritime Museum and Tourist Information Centre at the foot of Senhouse Street. This was the first plot of land to be developed by Humphrey Senhouse II, Lord of the Manor and builder of the town, which he named after his wife, Mary. The museum building, open throughout the year, was formerly the Queen's Head Inn; there is a profile of Queen Victoria in mosaic on the corner of the building.

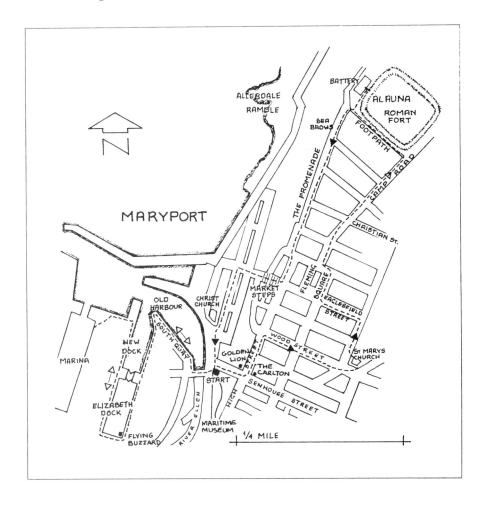

¤   Proceed up Senhouse Street, the town's main shopping thoroughfare. The Golden Lion Hotel, on the left, has hosted novelists
Charles Dickens and Wilkie Collins and the great railway engi-
neer George Stephenson, at the time when he was planning the
Carlisle and Maryport railway. At the junction of Senhouse Street
with High Street, the Italianate Carlton building, once a bank,
later a cinema, now stands sad and forlorn, facing the Town Hall
of 1890, which has fared rather better. Note the unusual style of
the columns on the High Street frontage.

¤   Turn left into High Street and then take the second turning on the
right, Wood Street. On the right, between Nos. 19 and 29A, is the
site of Whillens Yard. Here, Thomas Henry Ismay, founder of the
White Star shipping line, owners of the Titanic and other great
ships, was born in 1837. Ismay is by no means the only Maryport
resident to have had shipping and shipbuilding connections.

¤   Carry on along Wood Street to the Parish Church of St Mary. This
spacious sandstone structure was largely rebuilt late in the last
century. The churchyard has some interesting gravestone inscrip-
tions; on the far (East) wall is a plaque commemorating the
remarkable Joseph Peel, who died after a fall from his horse at the
age of 106. It is claimed that the horse took fright after being
scratched by a cat. The plaque lists the eight monarchs whose
reigns Peel's life spanned. If the church is open, it is worth seeking
out the wall mosaic depicting St Martin on his horse, some good
oak carving, and a contemporary sculpture by Josefina de Vasconcellos (see the Rydal trail, page 32).

¤   From the church turn right to walk up Church Street as far as
Eaglesfield Street. Turn left here to Fleming Square, formerly the
market place. Bounded by attractive Georgian and Victorian
houses, the square has been restored in recent years. Turn right
and continue uphill along Camp Road. Part way along, on the
right, is Christian Street, named after Fletcher Christian, of mutiny on the Bounty fame, another seafaring Maryport resident.

¤   Just beyond the last house on the left (Ellesmere), turn left into a
footpath signposted "Sea Brows". The path follows the line of the

boundary of the Roman fort of Alauna, an important link in the coastal defensive system which complemented the better known Hadrian's Wall. The site of the fort is now a close-cropped grassy meadow, but the defensive ditches and the depression which marked the south west gate can be clearly seen over the wall.

¤ At the end of the path turn right to the substantial building known as the Battery, once a Royal Naval Reserve Station. The Battery is now a museum, open every day from July to September; Tuesday, Thursday, Friday, Saturday and Sunday from April to June and in October; Friday, Saturday and Sunday from November to March (charge made). The museum has a fine collection of Roman sculpture, particularly the Romano-British altars discovered locally in the 19th century and assembled by the Senhouse family. Return towards the town by the Promenade, which has long views, and seats to enjoy them, across to Scotland, including Criffel and the Mull of Galloway. On a clear day the Isle of Man can also be seen. Stay close to the cliff top until the top of Market Steps, a flight of no less than 109, is reached. Descend the steps, go straight on at the bottom across Nelson Street, and turn left at King Street towards Christ Church, another Victorian structure. In front of the church is a large anchor, fished out of the Solway by a local boat; it is dedicated to Maryport seafarers lost at sea.

¤ The starting point at the Maritime Museum is now close. However, if time permits, turn right to cross the road bridge to South Quay, and bear right along the side of the Old Harbour. Incidentally, there is plenty of pay and display car parking along the quay-side. As the promontory is reached, turn sharp left and follow the roadway, firstly beside the Campbell or New Dock (1836) and then Elizabeth Dock (1857), Cumberland's first non-tidal dock, with gates controlled from the small brick buildings still evident on either side of the dock. At the height of the 19th century coal trade, these docks were a hive of industry, served by railway lines along the sides.

¤ At the end of Elizabeth Dock is moored the "Flying Buzzard", a restored Clyde-built steam tug of 1951, now equipped as a floating museum, open during the season only (charge made). The trail may be further extended by continuing along the far side of Elizabeth Dock, passing the site of the former lifeboat station, to reach Senhouse Dock (1884), biggest of all the Maryport docks, with an area of 6 acres. In 1989, the present marina was opened at this dock. The same route is used to return to the starting point.

The Flying Buzzard

15. Cockermouth

Description

L ying just outside the boundary of the Lake District National Park, Cockermouth is an attractive place, a real "Cumberland" market town not overwhelmed by the tourism atmosphere which so affects, for example, Keswick and Ambleside. Although on the fringe of Lakeland, the situation at the end of Lorton Vale does, in fact, give good access to the north-western group of fells.

Within the town, the wide and tree-lined Main street is quite gracious and, together with the adjacent Station Street, is provided with well-varied shops, inns, and other refreshment houses, by no means all tourist orientated. The River Cocker joins the River Derwent just below the castle mound, and there are several places with easy access to the banks of the rivers. Inevitably, there are odd waste sites and run-down buildings, but improvements do seem to be taking place and, on the whole, the town is very presentable.

The Romans built the fort of Derventio at what is now Papcastle, about one mile north-west of the present town centre, at a meeting place of the roads connecting Maryport, Carlisle, and Penrith. Cockermouth Castle was first built in the mid-13th century, but little of this earliest structure remains. The great majority of today's ruins date from 1360 to 1370, and the castle played a considerable part in the centuries of sporadic border warfare, becoming the focal point of the medieval town. The town received its market charter in 1221 and has since retained its importance as a market centre. The present market day is Monday.

Quarrying, and mining for lead and iron, were later developments outside the town and a sizable brewery has been constructed by the confluence of the two rivers, at the foot of the castle mound. The Cockermouth, Keswick and Penrith Railway was opened in 1864, primarily to provide for traffic to and from the rich industrial areas of the Cumberland coastal strip, but with a passenger service most useful for Cockermouth. Unfortunately, the line was closed in 1966.

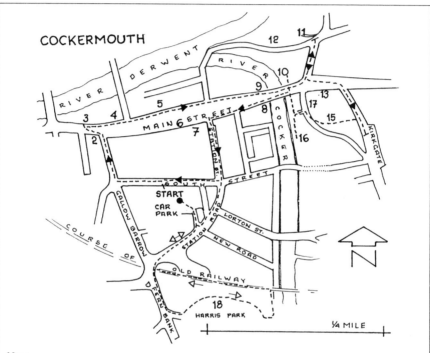

Key:

1. Christ Church
2. Wordsworth Bust
3. Trout Hotel
4. Wordsworth House
5. United Reform Church
6. Earl of Mayo
7. Globe Hotel
8. Midland Bank
9. Old Courthouse

10. Toy and Model Museum
11. Castlegate House
12. The Castle
13. Market Bell
14. Houses in Kirkgate
15. All Saints Church
16. Former Town Hall
17. Plaque to Mary, Queen of Scots
18. Statue

The Trail

The large and well-signposted pay and display car park on South Street, just behind Main Street, is a good place to start. Turn left along South Street towards Christ Church, a large building of 1865, with an sturdy tower. Turn right at Sullart Street towards Main Street. Facing is Wordsworth House, generally regarded as the best house in Cockermouth, and now in the ownership of the National Trust. (open 1st. April to 31st. October daily except Saturday and Sunday, 11am to 5pm). William's father John Wordsworth was land agent to the powerful Lowther family, moving into this house in 1766. Both William and Dorothy were born here, leaving on the death of their mother in 1778. John Wordsworth died in 1783.

¤ Before crossing the road, don't miss the William Wordsworth bust in its little enclave on the left. "William Wordsworth 1770 – 1850". At the mini roundabout, turn left into Crown Street. Across the road is the attractive Trout Hotel, with the Derwent Gallery/Mineral Museum adjacent. Opposite the hotel, another good building is the early 19th century house known as Grecian Villa. Return to Wordsworth House.

¤ Beside the House is a National Trust shop, then the Printing House, a working museum of printing (open Monday to Saturday, 10am to 4pm). Bridge Street leads to a footbridge over the river, with views to the castle and Jennings Brewery. A little further along Main Street, the United Reformed Church has a rather unusual frontage, with pinnacles. Across the road an alleyway by the Bank Hotel leads into the shopping precinct of Lowther Went.

¤ The centre of Main Street is dominated by the Earl of Mayo, or rather by the impressive statue to this local 19th century celebrity. Born in 1822, he was Member of Parliament for Cockermouth from 1857 – 67, then Viceroy of India from January 1869 until his assassination in the Andaman Islands in 1872. Opposite the bottom of Station Street, High Sand Lane leads to the confluence of the two rivers, with a footbridge to the brewery site. Across Main Street is the Globe Hotel, with a plaque recording associations with R.L. Stevenson and John Dalton, but the hotel achieved more recent fame for its part in the television version of Melvyn Bragg's novel "A Time to Dance".

¤ As the road rises to cross the River Cocker, on the left is the Old Court house, with the huge sandstone Midland Bank opposite. From the bridge there is a fair view towards the castle, including one tower which is leaning considerably. The Market Place is a few yards further. To the left is Banks Court, an alleyway leading to the Cumberland Toy and Model Museum (open every day from 10am to 5pm, but closed in winter). A short walk up Castlegate leads to the Art Gallery and to the castle entrance. Unfortunately, as the site includes a dwelling, the castle is not open to the public. There are good, if somewhat shabby houses along the street. The well-proportioned Castlegate House is at the top.

¤ Back at the Market Place, turn left. At no. 7, now a Chinese take-away, the old market ("butter") bell which was rung to signal the start of trading, sits in a recess at first floor level. Turn right into the narrow opening of Kirkgate, passing the Bitter End Inn, which brews in-house and claims to be Cumbria's smallest brewery. The street opens up to reveal a pleasant terrace of houses sitting behind horse chestnut trees and a cobbled forecourt.

¤ Return for a few yards and turn left through a gate into All Saints churchyard. All Saints was attended by the Wordsworth family but was unfortunately burnt down a few months after William's death in 1850. The present church, built in 1852-4, is believed to be the third on the site and is of impressive size, with a tall spire. There is a memorial window to the great poet, whose father, John, is buried in the churchyard. Adjacent was the former Grammar School, now demolished, attended by William from 1776-7; a fellow pupil, some years earlier, was Fletcher Christian of" Mutiny on the Bounty" fame.

¤ From the church descend the footpath to the smallish car park by the Town Hall below. This building started life as a Methodist Chapel, became the local Town Hall and, latterly, the area office for Allerdale District Council, including the Tourist Information Office. Two stone lions, of dubious quality, guard the entrance. In the car park is a simple stone pillar with a plaque recording a visit by the unfortunate Mary, Queen of Scots. On 17th May, 1568, she was received, as a refugee after defeat in battle, at a house named Fletcher Old Hall which stood upon this spot. The area can still be accessed by an alleyway called Old Hall Went.

¤ The Trail can now be terminated by returning to the Market Place, Main Street, Station Street, South Street and the car park.

¤ One further short excursion is recommended. Continue up Station Road, past the War Memorial and the Fire Service Headquarters. Turn left at Fern Bank and left again into Harris Park, small but well-kept and with views to the mountains. There are plenty of seats and the park is a good, quiet, place for a relaxing picnic at the end of the Trail. Of particular interest is a delightful small statue in memoriam of the childhood of William and Dorothy Wordsworth. Leave the park at the far side, down a long flight of steps, go left at the bottom to reach a broad track. On the right is the bridge which carried the railway high over the River Cocker. Turn left along the former railway line, pass the Fire Headquarters, and turn right at Station Road. Cross the road and turn left into the car park.

16. Keswick

Description

As principal market town of the northern part of the Lake District and so-called "Queen of the Lakes", Keswick ("cheese town") is a busy place in season, with a good shopping centre not entirely given over to tourist requirements. The town has a wonderful situation between Skiddaw, its own mountain, and the tranquil expanse of Derwentwater. Most of the town centre buildings are 19th century and are not particularly distinguished. Overall, the town never seems to be quite as attractive as it should be, although the general bustle around the Market Place, with plenty of colourfully clad mountain walkers in evidence, is quite appealing. Perhaps there are too many car parks occupying large tracts of land much too close to the heart of the town.

The oldest part of the settlement is at Great Crosthwaite, with the splendid church of St Kentigern, about half a mile from the modern town centre. The original church here is claimed to have been founded in 553 A.D., later becoming part of the vast area controlled by Fountains Abbey. Sheep farming was predominant for several centuries and Keswick became a great wool centre. A market charter was granted in the 13th century.

During the latter part of the 16th century industry was superimposed. Queen Elizabeth formed the Company of the Mines Royal in 1564, following which the Goldscope Mine in the nearby Newlands Valley was opened by German miners experienced in this type of work. The miners made their home on Derwent Island. The original hope was that marketable quantities of gold would be found, but it was soon realised that there was no gold, but rich deposits of copper. Other mines were opened in Newlands and at Caldbeck, furnaces were built at Keswick, and a great deal of woodland was cut down to provide charcoal for the furnaces.

As the copper mines faded somewhat in the mid-17th century, graphite was discovered and extracted locally, particularly around Seathwaite, in Borrowdale. This valuable mineral had a variety of uses but soon became the foundation of the world's first pencil industry. Mining around Keswick continued to ebb and flow until the 20th century.

No doubt because of its fine setting, in the second half of the 18th century Keswick became Lakeland's first true tourist resort, visited and extolled by most of the noted early travellers of the Romantic era, such as Dr. John Dalton, John Brown, and Thomas Gray. These were followed by literary figures, mainly poets, who made the district their home. Most notable were Coleridge, Southey and Shelley, with frequent visits from William Wordsworth himself. Thus was born the collective phrase "Lakes Poets", still in use today. Inevitably, the great and the famous were followed by lesser mortals, the tourists, the "trippers", arriving in droves at the station on the railway line, newly opened from its connection with the main line at Penrith in 1865.

In and around the town of today, there is plenty of interest including three museums, a swimming complex, a cinema (summer only), a theatre, and plenty of outdoor sports. All will be revealed in the trail set out below. Rowing boats may be hired on Derwentwater and the scheduled launch service around the lake is most useful for incorporating into walking excursions. Keswick is claimed to have more visitor accommodation right across the range, pro rata, than anywhere else in Britain; tea shops and other informal eating places proliferate. Although the railway line has, sadly, been closed since 1972, there are useful bus services to other Lakeland towns and along the Borrowdale valley.

Because this is a longer than average trail, it is suggested that, if time is short, the visit to Great Crosthwaite could be omitted from the walk and a vehicle used to drive to the church. In this case, from the Keswick museum a route across the playing fields to a foot bridge over the River Greta would give access to the bottom of Stanger Street, Greta Hall and the Pencil museum.

The Trail

The large pay and display car park between the town and the lake (follow the signs for the lake) is suggested as a starting place.

¤   The Century Theatre stands beside the car park. Believe it or not, this ramshackle collection of rather flimsy boxes did, for many years, roam widely among the towns of the north of England as a travelling theatre. Its eventual expiry on to the present site was presumably due to the difficulty of keeping the whole outfit roadworthy and the apparently horrendous job of setting up and taking down at each venue. Possibly Highway and/or Police authorities also had something to say – or perhaps it just failed its MOT! Anyway, the end of the road has been Keswick's gain, as this popular theatre is held in considerable local esteem.

¤   From the car park head towards the town, passing the pitch and putt, putting, and crazy golf. By a refreshment kiosk turn right at a signpost to go through a subway into Lake Road. A National Park Information Centre is on the right, immediately before the large building housing Fisher's long established emporium of mountain and other outdoor equipment. This building was previously the business home of the legendary Abraham brothers, pioneer 19th century climbers and photographers.

¤   Turn right, then immediately left into Derwent Street. Opposite the top of the street is "Open all Hours", with an interesting collection of old advertising signs on display, facing the Alhambra cinema. Turn left at St John's Street, then right into Station Street. Part way along turn left into Pack Horse Court, where fairly recent development has taken over the ground floor of the Royal Oak Hotel, famous for its associations with virtually all the Lakes Poets, Sir Walter Scott, and John Peel. The National Trust Beatrix Potter Experience is on the right (charge for entry, even to N.T. members).

¤   Turn right, to head for the "Cars of the Stars" museum, opposite the Court. Turn right to head back to Station Street. On the right

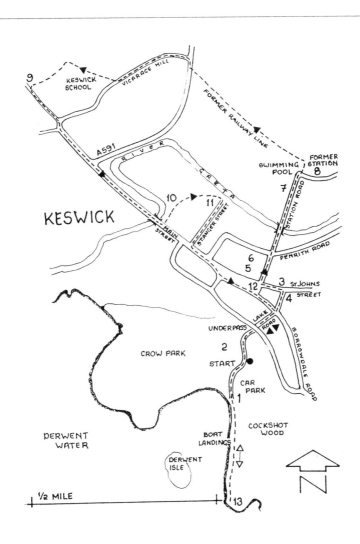

Key:

1. Century Theatre
2. Putting/pitch and putt
3. Open all hours
4. Cinema
5. Beatrix Potter Exhibition
6. Cars of the Stars
7. Keswick Museum and Art Gallery
8. Former Station
9. Gt. Crosthwaite Church
10. Cumberland Pencil Museum
11. Greta Hall
12. Moot Hall, Market Place
13. Friar's Crag

is Chaplin's bookshop, with a collection of photographs of famous authors displayed on the walls. From Station Street, Latrigg makes a pretty picture ahead. Cross the busy Victoria Street and continue along Station Road, crossing the River Greta and passing Fitz Park.

¤   The Keswick Museum and Art Gallery of 1879 (open from Good Friday to the end of October, Monday to Saturday, 10am to 4pm and on Bank Holidays) is next, with its charmingly "folksy" collection of local material, including letters of the Lakes Poets. From the museum continue along Station Road to the modern swimming complex constructed on former railway land. Pass to the right of the complex. Behind, to the right, is a surviving platform, with canopy, of the old Keswick railway station. The solid stone station buildings have been put to other use. Pass behind the swimming pool, along a residential roadway, then turn left at a kissing gate. Follow the track in the meadow to the right for a few yards, then turn right at a second kissing gate to rise to the former railway track bed.

¤   Turn left to walk along the line, with occasional excellent views of Skiddaw. As the track forks, keep left, downhill, soon arriving at a road junction. Turn right, pass the Pheasant Inn, and turn left to walk along Vicarage Hill, with a good view of Grisedale Pike ahead. On reaching the Lairthwaite site of Keswick school, turn right at a footpath signposted to Millbeck and Applethwaite. Follow this path behind some undistinguished school buildings, turning left at a corner to cross part of the school complex and arrive at Great Crosthwaite church, once the heart of ancient Keswick, but now quietly on the fringe.

¤   The churchyard entrance gate has the symbols of its founder St Kentigern – tree, bell, fish, and bird – displayed. The present building has just a little Norman work remaining from a previous church of 1181, but it is mostly of the 15th century, with a large scale restoration in 1844. Happily, the overall result is an attractive, dignified, and spacious church. Inside, among many items of interest, there is a well-carved 14th century font, and a striking white marble memorial to Robert Southey with the epitaph written by William Wordsworth, his successor as Poet Laureate. Southey, the legendary Canon Rawnsley, one of the three founders of the National Trust, and Jonathan Otley, the eminent early geologist, are all buried in the churchyard.

¤ From the church, cross the mini roundabout and follow the tree-lined driveway, with Keswick school above to the left, to the main road (B5289), turning left towards the town centre, half a mile distant. There is a good view of the north-west group of fells from this junction. Walk alongside, then cross, the River Greta. Turn left at Cardingmill Lane to the Cumberland Pencil Museum (open all year from 9.30am to 4pm other than Christmas Day, Boxing Day, and New Year's Day), part of the factory complex. The name of the lane indicates a former use of this riverside site.

Pencil Museum Van

¤ If you wish to see Greta Hall, continue along the lane, bending to the right beside the pencil factory. As the Hall is part of Keswick school, close examination is not possible, but the literary associations are so strong (Southey and Coleridge both lived here;

Wordsworth, Charles and Mary Lamb, De Quincey, and Shelley were all visitors, the former very frequently), that many will make this short diversion just for a peep at the Hall, which is on the right of the lane.

¤   After the Hall, pass along the backs of terraced houses as far as Stanger Street, turning right to return to the main thoroughfare. Turn left to reach the heart of present-day Keswick by the Moot Hall (housing the Tourist Information Centre) of 1813. Follow Lake Road to retrace the route to the car park.

Extension

If time and energy permit, an extension to the fine viewpoint of Friar's Crag is highly recommended. From the car park, the distance is almost half a mile.

Derwentwater from Friar's Crag

¤ Pass the Century Theatre, public conveniences, tea gardens, a National Trust shop, and boat landings to follow the road, then a well-worn track. Derwent Island is close by as a memorial tablet to Canon Rawnsley (1851-1920) is passed. As the track forks, keep right. Just before the promontory itself is an impressive upright stone commemorating John Ruskin, whose esteem has made the viewpoint particularly famous. Admire the extensive view and then return to the car park.

The Ruskin Memorial

17. Caldbeck

Description

C aldbeck is an attractive village with green and duckpond,
sitting in a shallow valley in the wide open spaces north of
Skiddaw and the Caldbeck Fells. Although the village is just
inside the boundary of the Lake District National Park, such is the
separation that it seems to have little in common with other towns
and villages in the Park or, indeed, with the Lake District generally.

The parish church is dedicated, like that at Great Crosthwaite,
Keswick, to St Kentigern (or Mungo), the 6th century Bishop of
Glasgow, and it is likely that an early church on this site was the
centre of a farming settlement. The present church building, fortunately attractive as a whole, embraces a greater than usual mixture
of dates and styles with, for example, a Norman entrance to the
otherwise much more modern south porch, some 13th century features, a great deal of the 16th century, and a number of Victorian
windows.

As early as the 13th century, mining commenced in the area around
Caldbeck. Lead, copper, wolfram and barytes have all been profitably
extracted over the centuries. In Elizabethan times, the German miners
re-opened several mines which were already old. Wolfram and
barytes were mined well into the present century, the last mine
closing in the 1960s. Closer to the village, the 17th and 18th centuries
saw industrial development of a more domestic type, with corn,
woollen, bobbin and paper mills all making use of the power provided
by the Cald Beck and its tributaries.

Despite its long and varied history, Caldbeck is best-known as the resting place of John Peel, a man whose claim to fame depends solely on a song with words conceived by a friend to a local tune or "rant", and later put to better music by the conductor of the Carlisle Choral Society. The mastery of a pack of hounds for more than 50 years and an almost exclusive devotion to the unremitting pursuit of foxes is, in itself, hardly the stuff of which legendary heroes are made. The story of the origins of "Do ye ken John Peel" are well-documented. The friend was John Woodcock Graves, who suggested the words while he and Peel sat snugly by the fireside in Graves's cottage, close to the Oddfellows Arms, chatting over hunting exploits while snow fell outside. Graves was the owner or manager of the mill at Caldbeck at which the coat of "Hodden Grey" was probably woven.

Hardly less well known is the story of Mary, "Maid of Buttermere", fleshed out in recent times in Melvyn Bragg's novel of the same name. Mary Robinson, widely known as a local beauty, was the teenage daughter of the keeper of the Fish Inn at Buttermere. She was unfortunate enough to be wooed, seduced, and married by John Hatfield, a remarkably plausible forty-four year old con-man of the early 19th century. Hatfield was already married, for the second time, and had deserted both wives and four children. His claims to be a member of parliament and to have titled connections were all false, and he had already spent seven years in prison for debt.

Hatfield married Mary in the name of the "Hon. Augustus Hope", posing as the brother of Lord Hopetoun. Unfortunately for him, a judge who knew Lord Hopetoun's brother challenged him. He was arrested, tried for forgery and, less than one year after his marriage to Mary, was hanged at Carlisle on 3rd. September, 1803. The case aroused great interest nationally, and even William Wordsworth went to talk to Hatfield while he was in prison in Carlisle. For a while, Mary became the heroine of contemporary ballads and plays, but later married Richard Harrison and passed the remainder of her life much more quietly as a farmer's wife, raising a family in Caldbeck.

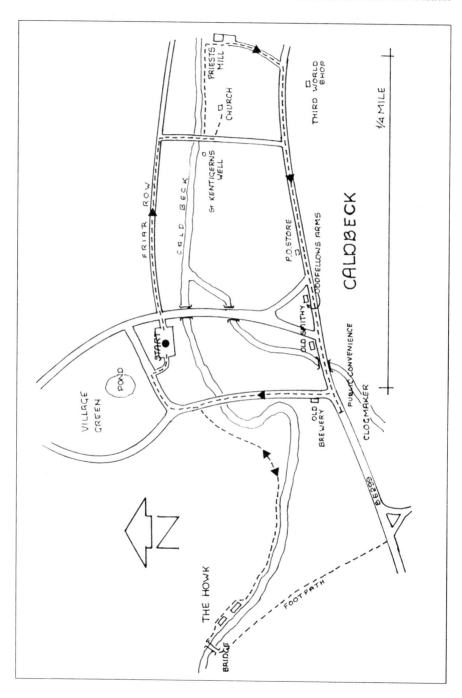

The Trail

The public car park is situated towards the west end of the village, beside the Cald Beck. Start here.

¤ Cross the B5299 road, to walk along Friar Row, with the beck on the right. Turn right to cross the beck by a packhorse bridge near the church. Across the water, on the right is St Kentigern's Well, down a few stone steps. Rather overgrown and not very exiting to look at, this very old well is dedicated to St Kentigern, who is reputed to have preached and baptised here following his flight from Glasgow in the 6th century, prior to the establishment of the first church on this site.

¤ Continue to the present church, also dedicated to St. Kentigern (or Mungo). Inside, note the difference in the arcade pillars. There is a fine font, some good glass, and a modern teak roof. On leaving the church by the south door, turn right in a few yards and walk towards the west wall of the churchyard to find John Peel's gravestone (1776-1854). Mary Harrison, together with her second husband and a fair number of other members of the family, is found a little further on, where a cross path

John Peel's grave

leads to a gate, again towards the west wall.

¤   Return towards the packhorse bridge, don't cross, but turn right along a beck-side path, reaching Priest's Mill in a few yards. Last used as a mill in the 1930s, this building has been tastefully restored and now houses a craft workshop, bookshop, and restaurant. Bear right, up to the road, and turn right to pass the Third World Gift Shop, the church, the post office/store/petrol station, and the Oddfellows Arms Inn, sole survivor of Caldbeck's total of six inns at the height of the 19th century industrial prosperity. Behind the inn is the Old Smithy, now a craft and tea shop.

Priest's Mill

Continue along the main road to the public conveniences and the workshop of the village clogmaker and boot and shoe repairer.

¤   Turn right, downhill, towards a long, low, house with an industrial chimney sprouting from the roof and the date 1671 on a door lintel. This building was a 19th century brewery, and probably an earlier fulling mill. Pass a nice house dated 1690 and cross the

Cald Beck to approach the large village green, complete with duckpond, but rather off-centre in its location.

¤ Before the green, turn left between farm buildings at a sign pointing the way to "The Howk". The Howk is an unexpectedly beautiful wooded glen, where the beck has cut deep into limestone, rushing over falls and rapids past the remains of a bobbin mill, where a huge water wheel once powered the machinery. The distance there and back is not much more than half a mile and no route finding is necessary. However, parts of the track can be muddy and there are some steps which need care.

¤ Return to the village green, walk along the bottom edge, and turn right into the car park.

18. Carlisle

Description

Quite small as a city, Carlisle is, nevertheless, huge by Cumbrian standards, a shopping, commercial, and industrial centre serving both the northern half of the county and a fair slice of southern Scotland. Not very many years ago Carlisle was considered to be such a dull place that a town trail would have had little appeal. Although, inevitably, there are still poor areas, changes in recent years have been generally beneficial, and the city is now a pleasant place in which to spend time and, possibly, money.

What has never been in doubt is Carlisle's strategic and historic importance as a border city; in fact, the border city. The Romans established the settlement of Luguvallium here, primarily to serve the nearby forts on Hadrian's Wall. After the Roman departure, Carlisle may well have been the capital of the rather shadowy kingdom of Rheged. During the later "dark ages" the city became part of the Anglian kingdom of Northumbria, then part of the British kingdom of Strathclyde, which expanded southwards then, after considerable Scandinavian settlement, it was annexed by Scotland. A period of see-sawing between England and Scotland was terminated by the Norman invasion, although it was not until 1092 that King William II captured Carlisle and asserted English domination by building the first castle.

Apart from the period from 1135 to 1157, when Stephen allowed the Scots to return and King David I is reputed to have built the present keep of the castle, Carlisle has since remained very much an English city. During the ensuing 500 years or so of periodic Border conflict, because of its vulnerable position Carlisle was always in the forefront, its mighty defences constantly being strengthened to repel the marauding Scots. The end result was a huge and powerful fortress, much of which remains today. Mary, Queen of Scots, was imprisoned here in 1568, before her removal to Bolton Castle. The castle played its part in the Civil War, changing hands three times and, for the last time, was taken in somewhat dubious circumstances by Bonnie Prince Charlie on his futile march to capture the throne in 1745. The city was also defended by strong walls, a portion of which, on the west, still survives.

Very early in the 12th century, King Henry I allowed the founding of a religious establishment at Carlisle for Augustinian Canons, later making the town the See of a Bishop. A great cathedral church was accordingly constructed during that century, with much rebuilding after a fire in 1292. The material is a reddish sandstone, with the exception of some dark grey stone in the earliest parts. Large scale restoration was carried out in 1853-7. The present structure has lost the greater part of the original nave, destroyed by the Scots in the 17th century and is, therefore, small by Cathedral standards. It is, however, full of interest.

Again because of the strategic position, Carlisle became a great 19th century railway centre with no less than seven independent railway companies sharing the use of the Citadel Station, and with extensive goods yards and locomotive depots on the fringes.

Tullie House, originally a 17th century town house, has been enlarged and adapted to become one of the finest provincial museums in the country.

The Trail

The huge pay and display car park at Devonshire Walk, north of the ring road and beside the castle, is recommended.

¤ From the car park use the underpass 100 yards or so to the left to cross the ring road. At once, Tullie House beckons and, subject to time availability, a visit should not be missed. (open Monday to Saturday, 10am to 5pm, Sunday 12 noon to 5pm). From Tullie House, continue through to Abbey Street, which has largely unspoilt Georgian buildings. Turn left to the top of the street, then right to West Walls. This road runs along the top of the remaining part of the old city wall, overlooking a large car park and the main railway lines. Continue along West Walls to the Tithe Barn, a restored 15th century barn close to the Cathedral complex.

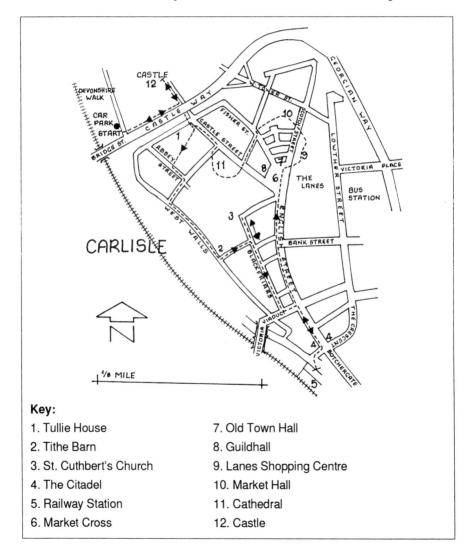

Key:

1. Tullie House
2. Tithe Barn
3. St. Cuthbert's Church
4. The Citadel
5. Railway Station
6. Market Cross

7. Old Town Hall
8. Guildhall
9. Lanes Shopping Centre
10. Market Hall
11. Cathedral
12. Castle

¤ Turn left here, then left at Blackfriars Street. On the left is St Cuthbert's Church, originally contemporary with the Cathedral, but now an 18th century structure, housing a unique movable pulpit. Head south along Blackfriars Street and, on reaching a main street, turn left, then right along English Street towards the Citadel. The present massive drum towers date from 1810, being replacements for towers constructed in 1542 on the orders of King Henry VIII.

The Citadel

¤ Just a little further, to the right, is the railway station of 1847, perhaps not quite what it was in the great days of steam, but still providing a wide range of passenger services and displaying the coats of arms of three of the original companies on its impressive façade.

¤ Return north along English Street, passing the statue of James Steel, Mayor of Carlisle 1845/6, outside Littlewood's store. The large and attractive concourse, with trees and largely traffic-free, is Greenmarket, with a market cross of 1682, a replacement of an earlier cross. Facing is the Old Town Hall, dated 1717, and housing the Tourist Information Office. To the left is the much older Guildhall, originally a town house named Redness Hall, and later the meeting place of the eight trade guilds of the city. The ground floor is now occupied by a restaurant, whilst the upper floor has a small local museum which closes during the winter. The building was renovated in 1978.

The Old Town Hall

¤   For a flavour of modern Carlisle shopping, turn right into The Lanes, circling back to Scotch Street, and then pass through the refurbished Victorian covered market. Turn left, then right to maintain the same direction as far as Castle Street. Cross the road to the Cathedral precinct, with its range of old and interesting buildings. Inside the Cathedral there are helpful interpretation boards, including a day by day account of the surrender to Bonnie Prince Charlie in 1745.

¤   Return along Castle Street to the underpass, facing the majestic bulk of the castle, which is open daily throughout the year (shorter hours in winter). Inside the castle is the regimental museum of the Kings Own Royal Border Regiment

¤   From the castle, return to the car park.

19. Wethrall and Great Corby

Description

Only a few miles to the south-east of Carlisle, Wethrall is a good sized village, with the main part standing high above the well-wooded valley of the adjacent River Eden. The village green is spacious and attractive, with two hotels, an inn, and a post office/store adjacent. Towards one end is a tall old cross. Just outside the village centre is a fine gate-house, all which now remains of the former Wetherall Priory.

Part way down the river bank is the parish church dedicated to the Holy Trinity, St Mary, and St Constantine, the last part claimed to be unique in Britain. Inside the church, the Howard Chapel has a superb sculpture in marble by Joseph Nollekens R.A. Along the river bank are three intriguing man-made caves, known as St Constantine's cell.

Wethrall railway station has survived, with services on the Carlisle to Newcastle line.

Facing Wethrall at close quarters across the Eden valley, Great Corby's principal distinction is the possession of a fine castle, parts of which may date back to Norman times. Like so many substantial old properties in Cumbria, a pele tower forms the core of the building to which many and varied extensions have been added over the centuries. Only the grounds are generally open to the public, during the afternoon, on payment of a small charge. As would be expected in this area, the village is largely constructed of sandstone, of particular interest being the former blacksmith's forge, prominent in the centre.

Communication between the two villages is facilitated by the pedestrian bridge attached to the viaduct which carries the railway across the Eden. Until the 1950s a toll of 1d (an old penny – of which there were 12 to 5 new pence) was levied for the use of this bridge.

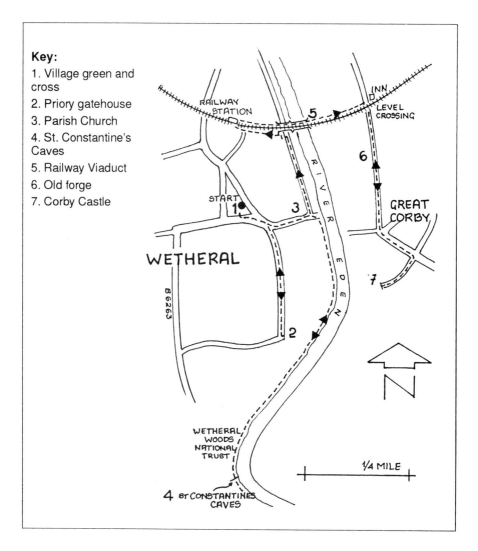

Key:
1. Village green and cross
2. Priory gatehouse
3. Parish Church
4. St. Constantine's Caves
5. Railway Viaduct
6. Old forge
7. Corby Castle

The Trail

Start at the village green in Wethrall, where discreet roadside car parking is possible. The tall old cross stands towards one end of the green.

¤ From here go left, then right to walk south along a narrow lane leading in a short distance to the remains of the Priory. The surprisingly well-preserved gate-house of the Benedictine priory founded about 1100 A.D., still stands and the adjacent farm probably incorporates some elements of the east range buildings. The gate-house is of the 15th century, a massive sandstone construction, with

Wetherall Priory gatehouse

the spiral staircase still usable to the second storey. There is an interpretation board on site.

¤ Return towards the green, but turn right, downhill at the road junction. The parish church celebrated its 800th anniversary in 1988, but the exterior is early 16th century, with restoration of the chancel late in the 19th century. The octagonal tower is also of the 19th century. Inside, there are 12th century arcades. The chapel/mausoleum for the Howard family of Corby Castle was added in 1791. Inside this chapel is the church's greatest treasure, the Nollekens sculpture. Poor Lady Maria, she was just 23 years old, married one year, when she and the baby died in childbirth in November 1789. The draped figure bending over Maria represents Faith. There is also a Nollekens statue of Adela Howard.

¤ From the church turn left to continue downhill to the river. Take the well-worn track to the right, a little muddy in places, as far as a short flight of steps. Ascend these and carry on, entering Wethrall Woods (National Trust). Go slightly left, downhill, at a fork and take care along the last section of the path as it finally descends a rather irregular flight of stone steps, without handrail. The distance to the caves is approximately half a mile, but the effort is well worthwhile. This is a superb section of the river valley and the caves themselves are cut into a sandstone cliff high above the water, giving fine views. On the far side of the river, along the way, some of the landscaped gardens of Corby Castle can be seen, falling steeply down the bank. There are three adjacent man-made caves and, whether or not the story of habitation by St Constantine is true, this is an impressive spot.

The River Eden

¤ Return to the bottom of the road in Wethrall but, below the church, turn right along a minor road. Before the railway bridge turn left to climb what is known as the "99 steps", up to Wethrall station. Not too many villages in Cumbria are privileged to have retained a railway passenger service. This is the Carlisle to Newcastle line of the former North Eastern Railway, completed in June 1838, the first line across England, and the first into what later became the great railway centre of Carlisle.

¤ Cross the station over-bridge and take the footway along the viaduct towards Great Corby, 600 feet long and at a height of 100 feet above the river.

¤ Turn right into the village, soon reaching the green and the curious exedra, built in 1833 as a blacksmith's forge, now a motor repair workshop. Continue to the castle entrance. If the grounds are open to the public (which is by no means always the case) and time is available, they are well worth a visit. The castle, which took its present form as late as the 19th century, is beautifully situated over the valley. The grounds were laid out over 250 years ago by Thomas Howard and include temples, a former cascade, and statuary including St Constantine, who faces the caves across the river.

¤ Return to Wethrall village green.

20. Penrith

Description

S trategically placed between the Lake District and the Eden valley, yet really belonging to neither, is the ancient market town of Penrith, with charter dating from 1223. Before the Norman conquest the town was the capital of the old Cumbria, closely allied to the Scottish Strathclyde. Its easy access from north and south brought the Romans and, nearly a thousand years later, several centuries of sporadic raiding by the Scots, not finally checked until 1603. The original defensive pele tower of 1397-9 grew into a sizable square castle, now only a meagre ruin, its stones looted as building material by 16th century vandals, as it was abandoned well before the end of that century. A visit by the Young Pretender, the west coast main railway line and, latterly, the M6 motorway, have all resulted from the same geographic considerations.

William Worsdworth and his sister Dorothy lived here for a while as children, attending a little school close by the church, where William first met his future wife, Mary Hutchinson.

Despite its historic and strategic significance, Penrith has remained a compact and friendly town. spared the worst excesses of tourism, a good mixture of old and new, with winding streets and yards, and some of the best of its sandstone buildings clustered around the parish church. Old signs distinguish several shops in which the same business has been carried on for up to two centuries, now supplemented by a small pedestrianised shopping area behind the Market Place and the modern Devonshire Arcade.

The Georgian parish church of St Andrew has the "Giant's Grave" and Giant's Thumb – ancient monuments – in the churchyard. Other features include a small museum attached to the Tourist Information Centre and a theatre.

"Giant's Grave" in St Andrew's churchyard

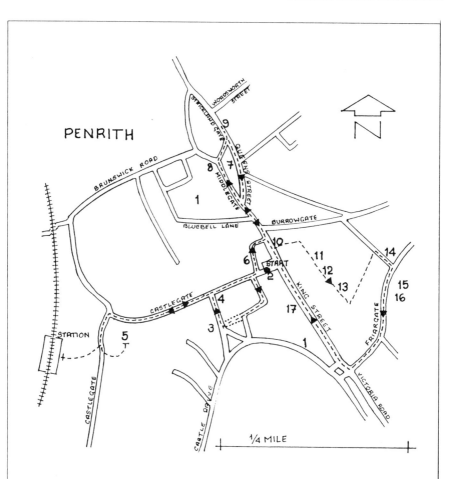

Key:

1. Car Parks
2. Market Square
3. Great Dockray
4. Cornmarket
5. Castle
6. Little Dockray
7. Tourist Information/museum
8. Musgrove Hall
9. Town Hall
10. George Hotel/Devonshire Hotel
11. Former Grammar School
12. St. Andrew's Church
13. Bishop Yard
14. Mansion House
15. Abbots Bank
16. The Friarage
17. Robin Hood Inn

The Trail

There are plenty of signposted car parks from which to choose. For a start at the Market Square, park as centrally as possible.

¤   In the centre of the square is the monument and clock tower of 1861. From here, walk past the handsome shop of James and John Graham, established 1763, into Grahams Lane, then Angel Square, passing through the pedestrianised area of modern shops attractively developed in a traditional style a few years ago.

¤   Turn right, then left, to reach the wide space of Great Dockray, used for the Tuesday market.

¤   Turn right. At the next junction is the Cornmarket, with the covered "Market Cross" building. There is no shortage of old inns and other refreshment places in the centre of Penrith. Turn left to ascend Castlegate, passing the small theatre then the former steam museum on the left. Continue left into Ullswater Road, and the entrance to the castle, perched on its mound in what is now

Penrith Castle

Castle Park. No charge is made for entrance to the ruins. The defensive ditch is most impressive, and the mound provides a good viewpoint.

¤ If railways are of interest, from the castle cross the road to the station. The Lancaster and Carlisle Railway (later the London and North Western, then the London, Midland and Scottish) built the main line over the famous Shap summit in 1846, Penrith later becoming quite an important junction, with connections to Keswick and Workington in the west, and over Stainmore to Darlington and the north east generally. As part of the west coast main line from London to Carlisle and Glasgow, Penrith still has a reasonable service, although the two connecting lines are long gone. The station buildings remain in fair condition.

¤ Return down Castlegate, then Cornmarket, turning left before reaching the Market Square into Little Dockray, an attractive backwater. At the far end a right turn reaches Devonshire Street, part of the main thoroughfare. Turn left to follow this street, which soon becomes Middlegate. On the right is the Tourist Information Centre and Museum, housed in the former Robinson's School, an Elizabethan building altered in 1670. The school use continued until the early 1970s.

¤ Opposite is Musgrave Hall, formerly the home of the family of the same name, whose coat of arms can still be seen over a defunct doorway. Continue by bearing a little to the right, to Stricklandgate and Corney Square. The large building on the right is the Town Hall which is, surprisingly, a 1905-6 amalgamation of two Adam style houses of 1791, one of which was the home of Captain John Wordsworth, cousin of the poet.

¤ Turn round and continue along Queen Street, home to several antique dealers. Bear right to angle back to the main street. Turn left to go as far as the George Hotel, used as lodgings by Bonnie Prince Charlie in 1745 on his ill-fated expedition. Turn left into the Devonshire Arcade, then right at the crossing point in the Arcade, to reach the St Andrew's Church precinct. Immediately on the right is the old grammar school building, dated 1564, now the public library.

¤ St Andrew's Church was established in 1133, but the oldest part of the present building is the 13th/14th century tower. The nave was rebuilt between 1719 and 1722 after a fire had damaged the earlier building. The architect is believed to have been Nicholas Hawksmoor, pupil and colleague of Sir Christopher Wren. The Georgian style, with its wide balconies, is certainly similar to several Hawksmoor churches to be found in the City of London. There is an interesting exposed clock mechanism near the west door. In the churchyard is a very fine and unusual monument made up of the remains of two stone crosses and four "hogback" tombstones, all pre- Norman.

¤ On the far side of the churchyard, to the south west, is the building which was the "dame" school attended by William and Dorothy Wordsworth in early childhood. Mary and Sara Hutchinson were fellow pupils. From here, walk along Bishop Yards, with a fine row of Georgian houses. Beyond the end of Bishop Yard is the Mansion House of 1750, now the main office of Eden District Council.

¤ Turn towards Friargate. Across the road is Abbots Bank, a large Georgian house of 1820, on the site of a 13th century chapel of an Augustinian priory. Next door is the Friarage of 1717, on the site of the house of the grey friars. Turn right to walk down Friargate, bearing right towards the main road, here named King Street. Turn right to return to the Market Square, passing the Robin Hood Inn, where William Wordsworth nursed a sick friend during a stay in 1794/5.

21. Appleby in Westmorland

Description

For centuries, Appleby had a strategic importance dispropor-
tionate to its modest size. Romans, Saxons, and Normans all
passed to and fro along the Eden valley and, more recently, for
more than one hundred years Appleby was the county town of the
former Westmorland, served by the Scottish main line of the old
Midland Railway.

Now by-passed by the busy A66 road and demoted by the 1974
reorganisation of local government, Appleby is a less important place,
just a tiny but beautiful market town (Royal Charter 1174),in the wide
valley of the River Eden, a long way from anywhere of importance
with high moors to the west and even higher Pennine hills to the east.
Once each year the town erupts into colourful life as the Gypsies and
other travellers gather in June for the Appleby New Fair, biggest of
its type in the country.

The Trail

The signposted car park at Broad Close just to the west of the town centre is very convenient as a starting place. Walk along Low Wiend to the Low Cross at the foot of the main street. On the left are the "cloisters", built around 1700 and rebuilt in 1811, to house the butter market. The cloisters provide a most attractive entry to the churchyard.

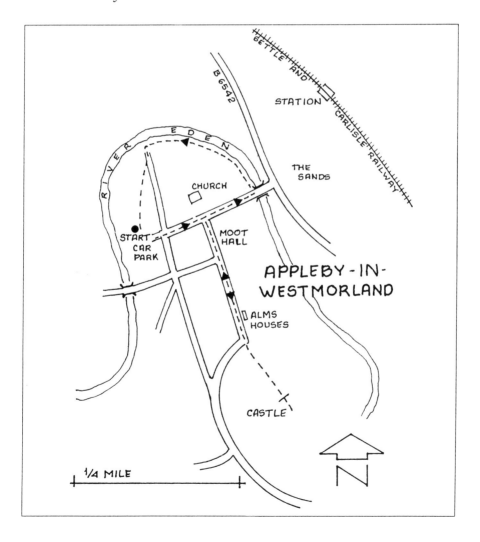

¤   The sandstone built parish church of St Lawrence is of 12th century origin but has had a good deal of reconstruction, not least because of two burnings by marauding Scots. The fine organ, allegedly the oldest such instrument still working in England, was a gift from Carlisle cathedral in 1683. Note also the comparatively comfortable elegance of the pews at the front of the nave, provided for the former Appleby Corporation.

¤   In the north east chapel are two elaborate monuments. One commemorates the redoubtable Lady Anne Clifford, the other her mother Margaret, Countess of Cumberland. Lady Anne Clifford was born at Skipton in 1590. She spent much of her life fighting to achieve recognition of her inheritance of the family land and fortune. Having withdrawn from Court to her northern estates, she set about rebuilding castles such as Brougham, Brough, and Appleby, to a large extent in defiance of the wishes of Oliver Cromwell, Lord Protector at the time.

Appleby church

¤   At the age of seventy, she celebrated the coronation of King Charles II, the restoration of the monarchy, by attending service in this church and then making public proclamations at each end of the town, from specially constructed platforms hung with cloth of gold. The journeys of this vigorous and determined woman between the centres of her various northern estates have become almost legendary.

¤ Return through the cloisters and continue up the main street. The Moot Hall, dated 1596, is still used for Council meetings and also now houses the Tourist Information Centre. The main street, Boroughgate, is regarded as one of the finest in the country. Of generous width and lined with lime trees more than 100 years old, it has great elegance. The houses and other buildings on either side date from the 17th to the early 20th centuries, but form a remarkably harmonious whole. The Red House, of 1717, was built as the Judge's lodging for the Appleby Assizes.

¤ With a certain inevitability, Boroughgate rises to the castle, set back almost discretely on its defensive mound. Although it has been rebuilt since Lady Anne's time, the castle is still of considerable interest and is open to the public from April to October. Within the grounds is a collection of rare breeds of domestic animals and unusual birds.

¤ Return down Boroughgate. The cross prominent in front of the castle gates is the High Cross, carrying the inscription "Retain your loyalty; preserve your rights". Together with the Low Cross it defined the limits of the town market; at this end was the cheese market.

¤ In a few yards, on the right is St Anne's Hospital, built by Lady Anne in 1653 as an almshouse with twelve small cottages and a chapel, beautifully set around a central square, with fountain. Each cottage carries a Lady Anne coat of arms, carved in stone.

¤ At the foot of Boroughgate turn right to reach the road bridge over the River Eden, with good views up and down stream. Across the river is the Sands area of the town, mainly 19th century. Most important here is the Settle – Carlisle railway, constructed through extremely difficult country by the Midland Railway Company in the early 1870s. This line was of great importance to Appleby until well after World War II. Although its importance has since greatly declined, the line has been saved from proposed closure and is now a highly regarded scenic route, with a reasonable passenger service. Appleby station has always been of some significance and railway enthusiasts will no doubt wish to extend the trail by taking the footpath opposite the bridge, heading uphill towards the station.

¤ From the bridge, turn right by the public conveniences to follow a pleasant riverside footpath, bending steadily left and passing sports grounds before leading directly back to the car park.

Appleby Almshouses

22. Kirkby Stephen

Description

A rather straggling little town, set among fine Pennine scenery in Cumbria's other National Park – the Yorkshire Dales – Kirkby Stephen and its district are steeped in history. A few miles to the south, in the Mallerstang valley, source of the River Eden, stand the ruins of Pendragon Castle, yet another of the dilapidated fortresses restored by Lady Anne Clifford (see the Appleby trail, page 118). The alleged connection with King Arthur is, to say the least, questionable. Closer at hand are the prehistoric earthwork known as Croglam Castle and the ruins of Lammarside Castle.

In the mid-19th century, the North Eastern Railway built its line from Darlington to north Lancashire though Kirkby Stephen, soon followed by the Midland Railway Scottish main line, the Settle and Carlisle. The former closed in 1962 but, against all odds, the latter has survived, with reasonable passenger services. With regard to Kirkby Stephen, however, it has to be said that the station is one and a half miles from, and 300 feet higher than, the town centre.

Although the population of less than 2000 indicates village rather than town, Kirkby Stephen clings to the status conferred by its market charter of 1361, the market still being held every Monday.

The Coast to Coast long distance walk pioneered by the late Alfred Wainwright passes through the town and is commemorated by the naming of a fish and chip shop, a favourite refreshment stop for the celebrated walker and no doubt many others following in his footsteps.

The Coast-to-Coast fish & chip shop

The Trail

The basic town centre trail is a very short walk indeed and precise route guidance in finding the points of interest is scarcely needed. The walk can readily be extended, as suggested, should time and energy be available.

¤   The Market Square and the streets behind provide a reasonable amount of car parking; otherwise use the signposted car park to the west of the main street. From the Square, go through an alleyway, turn right then left to reach Frank's Bridge, an attractive footbridge over the River Eden, with grassy picnic areas.

¤   Return along Mell Becks, turning right to Market Street and right again to return to the Market Place. The main street has plenty of

interesting old buildings, including some good inns. Just before
the Market Square is the Tourist Information Centre, while from
the top corner of the square a lane, which becomes Stoneshot,
leads down towards Frank's Bridge. Stoneshot is built over tunnels which are believed to have been dug to provide shelter for
women and children during the Scottish raids which took place
during the mid-13th to mid-16th centuries.

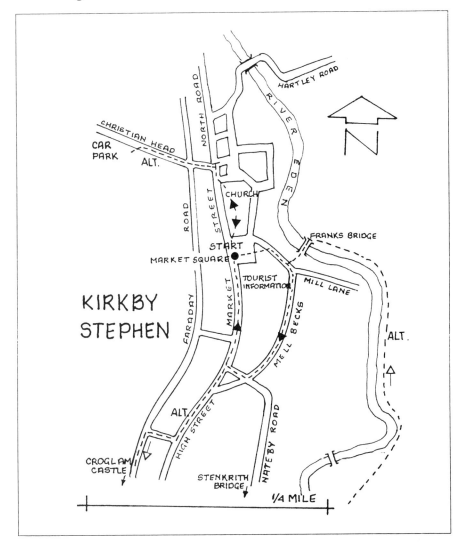

Frank's Bridge

¤   The area of cobblestones surrounding the square defines the area
     formerly used for bull baiting; apparently the "sport" came to an
     abrupt end after a bull broke loose in 1820! Most prominent on
     the north side of the square are the "cloisters", really an elaborate
     lych gate for the church, built in 1810 with funds left for the
     purpose by John Waller, a naval purser who was a Kirkby Stephen
     man. As at Appleby, the cloisters were used as a butter market.

¤   Through the cloisters, on the right is the Trupp Stone, where
     tithes were paid until 1836. The elegant parish church, known
     locally as the "Cathedral of the Dales", and built on the site of a
     Saxon church, is largely of the 13th century, with a sturdy 16th
     century tower. There are, however, relics of the earlier Christian-
     ity, most notable being a portion of a former Saxon cross, perhaps
     as early as 8th century, depicting a bound devil. This is known
     as the Loki Stone and is one of only two such stones found in
     Europe.

¤ From the church return to the main street. A little way to the right is the Coast to Coast fish and chip shop and the return to the public car park.

Extension

For a more extensive walk, the Croglam Castle earthwork is readily accessed half a mile to the south, starting along the main street, as is Stenkrith Bridge, a little more than a quarter mile to the east of the earthwork. By the bridge, the River Eden cascades beautifully among huge rocks. The return to the town centre can be along the B6259 road or, preferably, by a riverside footpath: start on the north side of the river and cross over to join a path leading directly to Frank's Bridge.

23. Sedbergh

Description

Sitting below the wild, high, moorland of the Howgill Fells, and close to the confluence of the Rivers Lune and Rawthey, is the tiny old market town of Sedbergh. Although best-known for its ancient public school, originally a chantry school founded in 1525, Sedbergh has a good deal to interest the visitor. The stone construction of most of the buildings is in general sympathy with the rugged local landscape, and even the main street had its original cobbled surface restored a few years ago. This restoration proved to be highly controversial and local pressure has recently resulted in the replacement of the cobbles by the more practical but less attractive asphalt. Along this street are shops, inns, tea shops, and commercial premises catering for residents and visitors.

The first market charter was granted in 1251, and the town later developed a thriving woollen industry, with both spinning and weaving taking advantage of the abundant availability of water power. The last mill, at Millthrop, closed after a disastrous fire in 1967.

Traditionally a Yorkshire town, included in the Yorkshire Dales National Park, Sedbergh was, nevertheless, transferred to the newly created Cumbria in the 1974 reorganisation of local government. Despite the proximity of the M6 motorway, just four miles along the Kendal road to junction 37, the town retains its "off the beaten track" feeling. Perhaps the demise of the modest railway service has something to do with this. Sedbergh is a fine centre for country walking (see, for example, the author's "Yorkshire Dales Walking – on the Level"), with the Howgill Fells to the north and Garsdale to the east.

The Trail

The free car park with public conveniences at Loftus Hill, at the Kendal end of the town, makes a good starting place.

¤   At the exit to the car park, the classical building on the right, dated 1716, is one of the oldest remaining parts of the famous Sedbergh School. Formerly used as classrooms, it is now the school library. Cross the road and walk down the passageway opposite, sign-posted "Cattle market or Busk Lane", for a few yards to a point from which there is a good view over some of the school buildings and playing fields. William Wordsworth's son was a pupil here, and Hartley Coleridge was a teacher until he was dismissed for excessive drinking.

¤   Return to the street, turn left then left again into the churchyard. George Fox, the father of Quakerism, preached here in 1652. St Andrew's parish church is a low, wide, attractively battlemented building, with some original Norman stonework, and many later alterations. There is a rather worn sundial over a small doorway in the south wall. Inside the generally pleasing and spacious church are memorials to famous Sedbergh people.

¤   Leave the churchyard by the lychgate to the main street. Immediately on the left is a 19th century shelter and reading room, now the public library. Pass this building to reach Evans House, a large mid-18th century residence, later the School House, named after a notable 19th century headmaster. There is a good Georgian door surround.

¤   Turn up Howgill Lane, opposite Evans House, passing attractive groupings of old buildings. At the top of the lane, set against the splendid backdrop of the Howgill Fells, are three pairs of large semi-detached houses, Highfield Villas. These houses, dated 1883, are claimed to be the oldest remaining shuttered concrete structures in Cumbria.

¤   Turn right at Bainbridge Road, which has trim little 19th century cottages along one side. In 70 yards turn right at a footpath

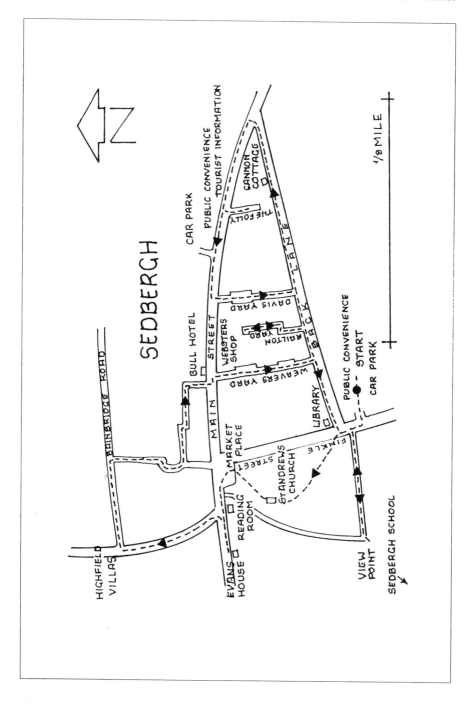

Main Street

signposted "Howgill Lane or Main Street". Twenty yards before Main Street, turn left to pass a furniture workshop and to sample the atmosphere of the alleys and yards behind Main Street, which were an important feature of life in Sedbergh in former times. Patches of cobble serve as a reminder of the appearance of Main Street until very recently – though it is worth noting that the cobbles were laid only a few years ago to add an "olde worlde" air to Sedbergh. Visitors loved them, but local residents hated them – so, no more cobbles!

¤   At the Bull Hotel, turn right to join Main Street. Across the road, a little to the right, is a small shop with overhanging upper storey. Dating from the early part of the 17th century, this is one of Sedbergh's few timber framed buildings which have survived the general change to stone as the primary local building material. Opposite the Bull, go down a narrow alley to Weavers' Yard, site of the town's first weaving looms. To the left of the alley is Webster's chemist shop, another 17th century structure. At the rear of this shop, the wide external chimney breast is reputed to have been the hiding place of Bonnie Prince Charlie before his escape in disguise back to Scotland after his failure to capture the Crown in 1745.

¤   Continue along the yard to Back Lane. Turn left and then left again in a few yards into Railton Yard. The house on the left, with mock Tudor bays, is Lupton House, a school boarding house. Higher up the yard are neat cottages with Sedbergh's last remaining "spinning gallery", unfortunately with rather too obviously renewed woodwork. As seen at Troutbeck (trail no. 4), these galleries were once a common feature in south Cumberland and Westmorland.

¤   Return to Back Lane and turn left, continuing to Cannon Cottage. Here, well-embedded in the ground, are two small cannons, reputedly abandoned by Bonnie Prince Charlie's men on their ignominious retreat to the north. Carry on to the road junction and turn sharp left into the end of Main Street. Walk towards the shopping area. On the right is the Yorkshire Dales National Park Centre. Opposite is a yard known as "The Folly", which retains much of the traditional residential yard atmosphere which the others have lost by demolition and/or change of use. A little further, opposite the public conveniences, is a house built in 1831 by a former head of the school. To allow the townspeople to continue to enjoy the view of the countryside, a wide arch was left open. It has since been closed by doors.

¤ Pass the United Reformed Church and turn left to Davis Yard, through a passage at no. 55 Main Street. By the entrance is another of Bonnie Prince Charlie's abandoned cannons. There was formerly a toll gate across this entrance, enforcing payment for the use of this short cut between Main Street and Back Lane. Proceed to Back Lane, now without charge, and turn right to return to the car park.

Index

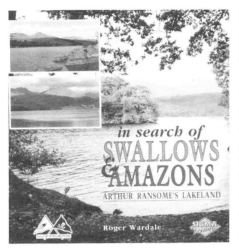

IN SEARCH OF SWALLOWS & AMAZONS: Arthur Ransome's Lakeland

Roger Wardale

This is a new edition of a popular book originally published in 1986. Additional material has been added to satisfy even the most avid reader of "Swallows & Amazons" – three decades of Ransome hunting with text and photographs to identify the locations of the ever-popular series of books. There's a two fold pleasure in this book – enjoying the original stories and discovering the farms, rivers, islands, towns and hills that formed their backdrop.

£7.95

WALKING LAKELAND TRACKWAYS: the Eastern Lakes

Mike Cresswell

These walks enable the reader to discover the historical significance of the paths, tracks and minor roads that crisscross the Lake District. In all, 24 well-planned routes that bring history vividly to life. Distances range from 6 to 16 miles.

£7.95

THE LAKELAND SUMMITS: a survey of the fells of the Lake District

Tim Synge

"A really workmanlike job" MANCHESTER EVENING NEWS

£7.95

FULL DAYS ON THE LAKELAND FELLS: 25 challenging walks

Adrian Dixon

£7.95

STROLLING WITH STEAM: Walks along the Keswick Railway

Jan Darrall

£4.95

100 LAKE DISTRICT HILL WALKS

Gordon Brown

"A useful addition to any walker's library" WEST CUMBERLAND GAZETTE.

£7.95

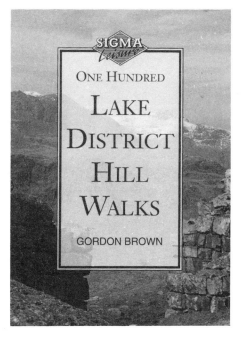

LAKELAND WALKING: on the level

Norman Buckley

"A good spread of walks" RAMBLING TODAY.

£6.95

MOSTLY DOWNHILL: Leisurely Walks in the Lake District

Alan Pears

"Perfect companion; thoroughly recommended" MENCAP NEWS.

£6.95

LAKELAND ROCKY RAMBLES: Geology beneath your feet

Bryan Lynas

Foreword by Chris Bonington

This is the companion to Snowdonia Rocky Rambles: "Refreshing ... Ambitious ... Informative ... Inspiring" – NEW SCIENTIST.

£9.95

PUB WALKS IN THE LAKE DISTRICT

Neil Coates

£6.95

CYCLING IN THE LAKE DISTRICT

John Wood

£7.95

All of our books are available from your local bookshop. In case of difficulty, or to obtain our complete catalogue, please contact:

SIGMA LEISURE, 1 SOUTH OAK LANE, WILMSLOW, CHESHIRE SK9 6AR

Phone: 01625 – 531035; Fax: 01625 – 536800; E-mail: sigma.press@zetnet.co.uk

Visit us on the World Wide Web – http//www.zetnet.co.uk/coms/sigma.press/

ACCESS and VISA orders welcome – 24 hour Answerphone service! Most orders are despatched on the day we receive your order. Please add £2 p&p to all orders.